# IS THE SWING HIGH OR LOW?

## LIVING WITH SOMEONE WITH BIPOLAR DISORDER

WILMA COTTEN

EXPLORA BOOKS
700 – 838 West Hastings St. Vancouver, BC V6C 0A6
www.explorabooks.com
Phone: (604) 330 6795



ISBN: 978-1-997587-43-9 (*Paperback)*
978-1-83430-121-1 (*Hardback)*

# Is the Swing High or Low?

# TABLE OF CONTENTS

# INTRODUCTION

I am writing this book as therapy to pour out all the pent-up feelings I have concerning my daughter and mental health. I want to emphasize in this writing that mental illness should not be looked at as being "crazy." It should not be shunned or looked down upon. It is, most of the time, a treatable illness, just like diabetes.

As parents, once our child is born, we have so many hopes and dreams for him/her. Will they be an athlete, prom queen, a musician, or an author? We rock them to sleep and sing lullabies, with all the joy and love our hearts can hold. We do the check-ups as pediatricians recommend, and pray these visits will go just fine.

What happens when all is not fine? That beautiful baby has juvenile diabetes and/or cancer. We do everything we can to fight whatever the disease is. Our hopes for our child to lead a normal life have been shattered. If we pray hard enough and do "all the right things," our child will continue to live a life as close to normal as possible.

But what if the diagnosis is depression or autism or ADHD? What do we do then as parents? We don't talk about it. We sweep it under the rug. We enter a stage of denial. What will other people think? We go through the stages of grief. How are we ever going to make our child better? The isolation sets in. Our peers don't understand what we go through. We are judged as bad parents. Why can't you make your child behave? Mental illness is just that—an illness, just like any physical disorder. It is an illness that, with the right medications and therapy, our child can lead a normal life. Every one of us needs to stop putting a stigma on mental illness.

Watch the news or look around you. Mental illness is everywhere. The mass shootings in schools. Those children needed help. They needed someone to listen and understand. They did not need to be judged as weird, or a nerd, or whatever other label had been put on them. They did not need to be bullied or neglected by their families. They needed to know where to reach out for help.

When I watch the news and see all that is happening to the younger generation with the mass shootings and the rise in teenage suicide, my heart just aches. It aches for the children themselves. It aches for the parents who are surprised and saddened by what their child did or suffered. And how could a parent not know what their child was thinking? Very simple, the stigma of having a mental illness is devastating to a teenager. The child tries to hide the feelings and symptoms. They often turn to drugs just to feel "normal." Many times, drug use starts with smoking pot. As a parent, with the push from society to do more and be more, we leave our children behind. That trend must stop. We must start putting our children first again.

Take time to play a game with them or just talk to them. Ask questions that are open-ended. Get rid of screen time. Don't let the cellphone you bought for them come between you and your precious child. Ask yourself, do I really know my child?

I make these points to make parents, grandparents, aunts, and uncles aware of how often the child in their life is asking for attention and looking for someone who cares. Someone they can trust and lean on. Be there, not just physically but really be there, at the moment. Practice active listening skills. I find many parents are in denial about what their child is feeling, so they dismiss it as a phase.

I am writing this book as a bereaved parent. A parent who has lost a child who had a mental illness. My beautiful firstborn daughter, Alisa, was taken from me in a very violent way. She had a mental illness: bipolar disorder.

The pain I feel every day will never go away until the day I take my last breath and leave this earth to be with her again. I want to share my experience and hers to educate society that mental illness is just that. No need to hide it or be ashamed of it. Society needs to be open and supportive of people with mental illnesses. Don't walk away from someone just because they seem "a little off." I am seeing a change in society's views, but it needs to happen faster. The new drugs that are coming out would have been so helpful to my daughter.

I do not want any other parent to feel the hurt and pain that I feel every day. It is isolating, debilitating, and paralyzing. Some days I can't muster the strength to wash a load of laundry. It is chronic fatigue, nightmares, anxiety, regret, and a sadness that you feel all the way to your toes.

# CHAPTER ONE

In order for this writing to make sense, I need to explain what Alisa's disorder was(is) for those readers who do not understand what the illness is and how it affects everyday life. I was devastated when Alisa was diagnosed. From that day on, life would never be the same. The following narrative gives me and my family's challenges with the disorder.

What is bipolar disorder? The following is quoted from WebMD: "bipolar disorder, also known as manic depressive disorder or manic depression, is a serious mental illness. It's a disorder that can lead to risky behavior, damaged relationships and careers, and even suicidal tendencies if it's not treated."

Bipolar disorder causes extreme shifts in mood. People who have it may spend weeks feeling like they're on top of the world before plunging into a deep depression. The length of each high and low varies greatly from person to person.

The two phases of bipolar disorder are the manic phase, consisting of periods of elevated or irritable mood accompanied by dramatic increases in energy, activity, and fast thinking, and the depressive phase, which includes a dramatic and deep depression.

A person may experience both the manic phase and the depressive phase at the same time or in rapid sequence. This is called rapid cycling.

If a person experiences four or more episodes of mania or depression in one year, they are rapid cycling.

When the individual is not treated and under control, the bipolar individual may have intense episodes of depression. Symptoms include sadness, anxiety, loss of energy, hopelessness, and trouble concentrating. They may lose interest in activities that they used to enjoy. It's also common to gain or lose weight, sleep too much or too little, and even think about suicide.

When someone is manic, the individual feels super-charged and thinks they can do anything. Their self-esteem soars out of control, and it's hard for them to sit still. They talk more, are easily distracted, their thoughts race, and they don't sleep enough. It often leads to reckless behavior, such as spending sprees, cheating, reckless driving, and substance abuse. Three or more of these symptoms nearly every day for a week, accompanied by feelings of intense excitement, may signal a manic episode.

Doctors don't know exactly what causes bipolar disorder. Current theories hold that the disorder may result from a combination of genetic and other biological, as well as environmental factors. Scientists think that brain circuits involved in the regulation of mood, energy, thinking, and biological rhythms may function abnormally in people with this disorder, resulting in the mood and other changes associated with the illness.

It affects daily life for both the individual and their families. When it's not under control, bipolar disorder can cause problems in many areas of life, including your job, relationships, sleep, health, and money. It can cause the individual to have trouble with drugs or alcohol. They may drink or abuse drugs to ease the uncomfortable symptoms of their mood swings. Substance misuse may be prone to occur as part of the recklessness and pleasure-seeking associated with mania. Committing suicide is 10-20 percent more likely in a person with bipolar disorder than in others. All these changes in mood and behaviors are incredibly stressful for the people who care but don't know how to help.

Bipolar disorder is one of the most difficult mental illnesses for families to accept, according to experts. When a person is sometimes very productive and then becomes unreasonable or irrational, it may seem more like bad behavior than an illness. Parenting a child with this disorder feels like you live your life walking on eggshells. You spend a lot of time wondering what you say or do will trigger an episode. Many patients will get help and start taking medication, only to quit taking the medication because they feel fine since taking it. It is a vicious cycle. When the child is over a certain age, they cannot be forced to continue taking their medication. All you can do, as someone who cares, is to try to convince the person to get help and hopefully, be successful. Otherwise, you stand by and watch the person slowly destroy themselves.

# CHAPTER TWO

When we are dating someone, all we feel is the giddiness of the courtship. Couples who marry after a very short romance can sometimes miss things that are a part of their partner. Rarely do couples talk about family history for any medical or mental illnesses that may be passed down to the next generation.

I was off to college and carried the baggage of small-town living within me. I had very low self-esteem. Having come from a small town in New York, where the area's mentality was if you were not married, engaged, or pregnant by the time you graduated high school, you were set to be a spinster. I dated in college. He was everything I had hoped for in a lifelong partner. He gave me a promise ring. We moved in together. I was very happy. A year and a half later, he broke things off with me. He married someone else. I left school.

I had moved to Columbus after leaving school, with encouragement from my sister Paula and her husband Tom. I had a two-bedroom apartment on the west side of town. I was working as a temporary employee for the state of Ohio until I got a job at Nationwide Insurance.

I need to mention that I take people at face value. I do not think people have ulterior motives. I am still surprised when I find out they do. I am an open book; what you see is what you get. Many people have told me I wear my heart on my sleeve. I guess that is why so many people have taken advantage of me over the years. It also explains why I let my daughter, Alisa, get away with so much.

My soon-to-be husband, James, was living with his parents since he had just returned from San Diego, where he had been stationed during his Navy career. His parents' house was on the east side of Columbus, a long way from my apartment. If I went out, I went out on Saturday nights while James' night out was Friday.

One Friday night, the girls I worked with suggested we have a girls' night out. When we arrived at the bar, it was busy. We got drinks and sat at a table kind of in the middle near the bar. Terri and Sue got up to dance while I watched the action and their purses.

In my naïve state of mind and with feelings of low self-esteem, when James approached and offered to buy me a drink, I was thrilled. He followed me home that night. I expected him to leave in the morning, but he did not. By the afternoon, I was very frustrated. I could not figure out how to get him to leave. I think he finally left because he had to work later that day. He was working in a gas station on the east side of town.

James and I had a short romance in the summer of 1984. He was ex-Navy who wanted to start a life by getting married and having kids. I worked as a claims processor for Nationwide Insurance. We met in February and got married in October that same year. I did not want to be a spinster. I married him because he asked. Looking back, I am not sure if I was in love with him or in love with the idea of being married. I do wish I had gotten to know him and his family more before I married him. I don't know if it would have changed my mind or not about getting married. After getting married, James threatened me. If I were ever to leave him, he would "hunt me down."

We announced in June that we were getting married the following spring. Sue (James' mother) got very angry. She said she couldn't plan a wedding in that short amount of time. Then she asked if my parents were going to pay for it. I told her the wedding would be what we could afford. I started planning while Sue continued to push us to do things her way. We finally got so angry at her that we changed the date to October. We sent her an invitation. Paula helped me plan. She and Tom had been married in a church with a pastor. Paula got in touch with him. He agreed to marry us in the apartment. Paula bought my dress. It was a white prom dress that was from the clearance rack at a local department store.

The wedding day came. We had set the time for 1 P.M. Sue and Richard (James' parents) arrived and brought some food and a wedding cake. This was a surprise. Tom was going to take pictures. Paula was my maid of honor, and Mitch (James' brother) stood up for James. The wedding didn't start until about 1:15 because we had to wait for James' Aunt Sue to show up. This woman was fashionably late to everything. I wonder if she was late for her own funeral a few years ago.

Paula was in the bedroom with me while I got dressed. Sue came in. "Do you really know what you are doing? We don't believe in divorce." She was questioning me about marrying James. It caught me off guard. It made me more determined to get married and make it last. We were successfully married by 2 P.M.

I did not question my future husband's family history. I was told that his paternal grandfather had committed suicide by hanging. In discussions of family history, most of the conversation was about his maternal side and how they grew up poor and separated from their parents. There were never any conversations about medical history or mental health issues.

Looking back at this time of my life, I know why I did the things I did, but I should have insisted on a longer engagement. I was feeling insecure, so I rushed into a marriage neither one of us was ready for. If you are engaged or planning on marriage, really get to know the person. You learn a lot about someone by watching how they treat restaurant workers and workers who do manual labor. Each person on this planet should be treated with dignity and respect. I have always treated people as I want to be treated—from the janitor to the CEO.

Also, pay attention to how their parents interact with each other and how those parents treat your significant other. When I was introduced to James' parents, his mother did not talk about James. She talked about her other son, Mitch. James was the black sheep of the family. The Smiths never showed affection for each other.

I did have a couple of visits with James' maternal grandmother, Grace. We went to her home in West Virginia once that I remember. Her house was crumbling around her, and her bathroom floor was about to cave in. She did not seem to be bothered by any of this. Her personality was very negative. She was an angry old woman who would argue with you about the color of the sky. We had a birthday party for her when she turned 75. During that afternoon, she kept insisting that I had permed Alisa's hair. According to Grace, no one could have hair that curly. I could not convince her that the hair was all natural. I thought she was just being a normal old lady, but later I learned that she had not been a good mother and had spent a lot of time looking for a new husband, leaving her children with relatives for long periods of time.

I am going to tell you about Grandma Grace's funeral here because she had very little interaction with James, me, Alisa, and Debbie. We drove to Parkersburg, WV, for the funeral. Alisa was about three, and I remember carrying Debbie. After we had viewed the body, which I did not allow either girl to look at, we went to find our seats. Alisa turned, looked at me, and said, "Can I pick my seat?" Her great-uncle Pat burst out laughing. I said to Alisa, "Yes, you may choose your seat." Out of the mouths of babes.

I am giving this background for the reader to have a better understanding of how I got to where I am. James knew I had a birth defect. A cleft palate cannot be hidden if you are a woman. Men can hide it with a mustache. James did not care about my birth defect. He just wanted to beat his older brother to the altar, so he asked me to marry him. He very seldom complimented me on my looks or anything else.

My parents weren't overly affectionate towards each other. Dad would kiss Mom goodbye when he left for work in the morning. When they did kiss, it was three kisses—always. They did enjoy square dancing together and would occasionally go out for a night of dancing. It was considered a normal 1960s marriage, I guess. Dad worked. Mom stayed home with us kids. Mom kept house and had dinner on the table every night at 6:15. I feel I had a warped sense of a true relationship. Wife does all the cooking, cleaning, and raising the kids while the husband brings home the bacon.

James had an even more warped sense of what a relationship should be. His parents never showed affection for each other. They existed in separate rooms most of the time. Richard in the kitchen and Sue in the living room. Many times, they were watching the same television show. With this behavior as an example, James was much the same way. We didn't hug or kiss very often unless he wanted sex. That was the affection I got most of the time. Without getting explicit about our sex life, sex was just that, sex, with very little foreplay and no afterward cuddling. He would immediately get out of bed and leave the room. I asked him once why he did that. "I get energized from sex and can't relax." Before marriage, sex was more intimate. I remember standing in the kitchen of the house, washing dishes and wishing in my head that James would come and put his arms around me. It never happened. This type of being shown affection was something I had had before, so I missed it a lot.

Mental illness can be hereditary, and after about five years of marriage, James' bipolar disorder began to show. I suspect that he got it from his grandfather. His attitude and behavior started to change.

# CHAPTER THREE

## *Early Years*

I had told James that before I would marry him, he had to find a better job or go to school. He went to school for programming and worked nights delivering pizzas. We basically lived on my salary. He got the better job and started making a lot more money. That did not help our financial situation, however. James' attitude was "I am making the money; I am going to spend it the way I want." He went so far as to go behind my back and ask his brother for a loan to buy a computer. We continued to live on my paycheck while he did what he wanted with his about fifty percent of the time.

I mentioned before that James had been in the Navy. He had enlisted for four years. When those four were up, he decided to reenlist for another four. The Navy gave him a bonus of $15,000 for reenlisting.

Upon reenlistment, James was placed under a new commander. There was no love lost between the two of them. The officer would be hard on James. James never said what "being hard on him" meant. He just called the guy an asshole. James started missing the ship's departure times. About two years into the reenlistment, James was being "harassed," as he put it, so he punched the officer. He went to the brig until the ship returned to port. From there, he was discharged. It wasn't a dishonorable discharge, but it wasn't honorable either. The Navy decided he didn't fit Navy life anymore.

We were about ready to celebrate our first wedding anniversary when a letter came from the Department of the Navy. It was a letter demanding that the $15,000 be repaid within thirty days. He tried to call and work out payments. That did not help. The Navy wanted $300+ a month until it was paid off. During the repayment time interest would accrue. We felt we would be paying forever. We could not afford that kind of payment since James wasn't done with school and was still delivering pizzas at night.

James wanted to file for bankruptcy. I did not. I had worked hard to build a great credit history. Credit scores were not used as they are now, but I could walk into a car dealership and walk out with a car without a cosigner or any issues. We declared bankruptcy. In those days, you could file for bankruptcy against the government. Today you cannot. I cried for days after making the decision. All the hard work of paying bills and getting my first credit card had been thrown away.

The less-than-honorable discharge from the Navy caused the bankruptcy, but it also had another consequence. James could not get veterans' benefits. Our life together was going to be dependent on insurance, same as everyone else. Having insurance benefits through the VA would have made life a lot easier.

Sue and Richard had always been critical of James. In Sue's eyes, he couldn't do anything right. Their son Mitch could do no wrong. Once we got married, Sue continued to try to run James' life, which meant she was trying to run mine. I had been on my own for a while so this became a point of contention.

We would have small get-togethers for birthdays, nothing big, just being together. James' birthday is September 11th, and his parents came by as usual. What was not usual was the conversation I had anticipated having with them. I was going to stand up for us. Sue started her criticism of James. I jumped in. I explained to them that James and I were adults. We could think for ourselves and make our own decisions. Sue tried to remain calm but Richard did not. He got up from his chair stating he didn't have to listen, and stormed out the door. Sue followed shortly thereafter.

James wanted to start a family right away. I wasn't ready to be a mother. I was only 23. James convinced me otherwise. The first time I got pregnant I had a miscarriage. Many women feel a sense of loss after a miscarriage. I did not feel that way. My thought process said it was not the right time to have a baby. In doing an examination of me after the miscarriage the doctor discovered I had an ectopic pregnancy (pregnancy outside of the uterus). I was supposed to have a routine procedure to take care of the problem. I went into the hospital thinking this shouldn't be too bad. The procedure would not include cutting me open.

I awakened after the procedure to find I had been cut open. The doctor had found that I had endometriosis. This disease is where blood collects outside of the reproductive system and causes pain and infertility. I also had an extra fallopian tube hanging out in my abdomen. I was cut open, and the lesions caused by the endometriosis were removed along with the extra tube. I was in shock about having had surgery. I did not know how to process this situation. James took me home to recover. I don't remember him taking care of me.

After recovering from surgery, James and I started trying again to have a baby. The doctor had advised that the endometriosis could return, causing me the inability to get pregnant. On my 25th birthday in 1986, we found out I was pregnant again.

We moved into a two-bedroom townhouse on the west side of town. During the pregnancy, I was very sick in the first few months. I would crave Mexican food, but if I ate it, I would get very sick. The smell of anything being cooked in a microwave made me sick as well. The good thing during this time, James and I had both gotten jobs at the same company, and we worked second shift. I would have morning sickness, and then we would go to work. I worried the whole time I was pregnant that the child would be born with the same cleft palate I had. I was so relieved when she came out perfect.

On October 2, 1986, I went into labor around 11 P.M. James drove me to the hospital about 3 A.M. Alisa did not make her appearance until 6 P.M. the following night. She was born on a Friday. After eighteen hours of labor, I was exhausted but so excited. James watched the birth, but I did not. She was taken and cleaned up while I was wheeled to my room and settled into bed.

I knew Alisa was special because she was the first grandchild for Sue and Richard. To show she was special, she was not crying or sleeping when they wheeled her into my room. She was humming. James' parents were there. I can still hear Sue saying, "Oh, I finally got my baby girl." Sue had two sons, no daughters. I corrected her by responding with "That's my baby girl." And so, the constant questioning of how we were parenting began.

As a new parent, I wasn't sure what I should be doing. I had helped with Henry (my baby brother) and lots of nieces and nephews, but to have one of my own was another story. Here James and I were with this tiny bundle of joy, and we could only guess what to do. No child comes with an instruction manual. I had read some books on early childhood development, which did help some. That is, until Sue started telling me what I should be doing. Sue would ask things like "Why don't you use cloth diapers?" and "Why don't you make your own baby food?" I did not breastfeed, and again, Sue was after me about that. I was working full-time. What Sue was challenging me about were things I could do if I were a stay-at-home mom. Sue's favorite line was "Why aren't those girls in dresses?" She used this line more after Debbie was born. This constant barrage of questioning our decisions felt like I was unable to care for Alisa. (Low self-esteem continued to build.) Since James had always been criticized by his parents, he did not take offense to these comments.

Alisa developed colic during her first few weeks, so I spent many nights walking the floor with her. One night, I was rocking her since she had just finished her bottle. James got on his knees to talk to her, and she vomited all over him. Not just a little, but projectile vomit. I chuckled under my breath. I felt it was payback because I was doing most of the parenting. I was the one who did the late feedings. It was harder to wake James so he could feed her than to just get up and take care of her.

I wanted to start family traditions with James and Alisa but that was not possible. We had to spend every holiday with the Smiths. That was fine with James because it meant he did not have to do anything but show up. After a couple of holidays, I gave up on the idea of family traditions. It became more defined after James and I got divorced. Since the girls had to spend holidays with their dad after the divorce, the dream of having any traditions with my girls was no longer a reality. As Alisa got older, holidays were something to be dreaded. Holidays can be stressful to an individual with bipolar disorder- the change in routine combined with the stress can be very disruptive to their sense of normalcy. Change affected Alisa in many negative ways.

Alisa was a very smart little girl. I had read the baby books about what a child should do at what age. Alisa was always ahead of the books. I felt like I had to run to keep up with her. I was continually talking to her. I would talk to her in a grocery store. Not baby talk. People would stare at me like I was crazy. I know they thought Alisa couldn't understand me. I knew otherwise.

During our time in the townhouse, I would prop Alisa up in a chair while I changed out of my work clothes. Again, I would be talking to her. I would read her bedtime stories. I did not sing lullabies because James said I was tone deaf and he did not want to hear me singing. We would put the side down on her playpen so she could climb in and out. That made her more mobile. She would crawl around behind one of us. When Alisa started crawling, James decided we needed a puppy. He brought home a little black dog and named him Pepper. I did not like dogs at all then, and we had a baby in the house. What was he thinking?

In January of 1987, three months after Alisa's birth, I was invited to a wedding of a couple I had known in college. Another friend was going, and she was driving right through Columbus. She called to ask if I wanted to go. Sure, I'll go. It would be nice to see college friends tie the knot.

After leaving the apartment, my anticipation grew. My college sweetheart would probably be there. Once I got inside the church, I saw that I was right. He was part of the wedding party. The familiar butterflies were back inside. I couldn't wait to talk to him. How was I going to let him know that I wanted to be with him and not James?

At the reception, Kevin came up beside me in the food line and started talking. I loved the sound of his voice. We went to a nearby table to eat. We talked as if we had never been apart. The room disappeared, and we were the only ones there. I asked about his marriage. He said she wasn't what he was looking for. I was hoping he would ask about getting back together, but he didn't. A little later, one of our other mutual friends came up and asked the question for him: "Are you two getting back together?"

Here it was, the question of the night. My second chance for happiness and I blew it. I held out my hand to show my wedding ring and said, "I'm already married." I did not say that I loved James. I had to make a choice—Kevin or Alisa? Kevin disappeared a short time later. I wanted to run out of there to find him, but I couldn't.

I know that people get divorced all the time. They remarry someone who has children. I think that was what Kevin was trying to tell me that he wanted to do, but I let my pride and stupidity get in the way of happiness. I have been conflicted ever since. I know I hurt him. I think about how happy I might have been.

On the flip side, after James had threatened to hunt me down and having a baby at home, I didn't feel I could leave. If I had left, I would not have had my miracle baby, Debbie. Realistically, I don't know if the love between Kevin and me would have been strong enough to fight James for eighteen years. Would Kevin have been able to be a parent to a bipolar child? As I reflect on it now, forty years later, I realize that by saying what I did, I allowed Kevin to find happiness in life. He is remarried with two children of his own. Isn't that what true love is—wanting the other person to find happiness?

I digress.

Living in a townhouse was not good enough for the Smith grandparents. Once again, the Smiths had to have their way. We were told by his parents that their grandchild was not going to be raised in an apartment. We had no way we could come up with the down payment to purchase a house, so Sue and Richard gave us the down payment. It was stated that we had to find a house that Sue and Richard approved of and that we would pay them back. We found a house on the east side of Columbus that his parents approved of, so in June of 1987, we moved into our first house. It was about a ten-minute drive from Grandma and Grandpa. I don't remember ever paying them back.

As we settled into the house, Alisa continued to amaze me with how fast she was learning. She started walking at nine months. We would use a marble coffee table to block her from going upstairs. She just climbed on the table and up the stairs she went. Her personality was really starting to develop. She was extremely active. She would yell and make silly noises. She had a hard time winding down at night to go to bed. Sue said we needed to keep her away from sugar because she might have attention deficit disorder.

I had gone back to work after five weeks of maternity leave. I cried all the way to work after dropping her off at the daycare. I got off work before James did, so I would pick her up on the way home. She and I would watch *Sesame Street* together while we waited for Daddy to come home.

Putting Alisa to bed at night was pretty easy after she got over her colic. We would put her in her crib with a bottle and walk away. Well, this started changing. She didn't want to go to bed. We would put her in bed, and she would cry. Sometimes for a long time. One night, we put her in the crib, kissed her, said goodnight, and left the room. This would be a long night of crying. She cried and cried. All of a sudden, it got really quiet. I went to check on her, and she was sitting on the stairs, grinning at me as if to say, "See what I can do?" We knew that she had climbed out of her crib, but we had no idea how. To this day, I have not figured it out.

During the summer of 1987, James and I installed a privacy fence around the backyard. We had an alley behind us and beside us. Then we had the street in front. It was less than a perfect yard for kids. When we finished installing it, James looked at me and said, "I built it. Now you get to stain it." He kind of chuckled. With Alisa in tow, I stained the fence by myself while trying to keep her busy and out of the stain. We received a notice from the city that we had to remove the fence for failure to obtain a permit to build it. James said he would handle it. He went before the city and got the approval to leave the fence up. I was relieved.

The yard had a big bush that produced some kind of berry. They were purplish in nature, but I knew they weren't blueberries. We decided the bush had to go. James chopped it down and then dug out the root system. Rather than just covering the hole, we decided to make the hole into a sandbox. What kid doesn't like to play in a sandbox or swimming pool? We finished it, and Alisa spent a lot of time there. The next time Grandma and Grandpa came over, Grandma started ranting about what a dirty thing the sandbox was. She insisted it was full of bugs and that we should not let Alisa play in it. We ignored Sue's objections to the sandbox. Alisa spent many happy hours playing with the sand. Eventually, Debbie played in it as well.

I got pregnant again in 1988. I went to New York to see family in May that year. I did not know I was pregnant. But Mom knew. She looked at me and asked what was wrong and why I was acting differently. I returned to Ohio and had a pregnancy test. I called to tell Mom. She said she already knew. That is one of my regrets— that I did not visit my parents more. Since money was always tight, I never felt like I could spend any to go see Mom and Dad. I was isolated from my family and drowning in his.

During the summer when I was pregnant, Alisa was so excited to think of having a baby of her own to play with. We did not have the gender revealed, so we could not tell Alisa that she was going to have a baby brother or a baby sister. We told her that she would make a great big sister, and she would have to play easy with the baby.

During the pregnancy, all I craved were tomatoes, cucumbers, and green peppers with Italian dressing. I had so much energy. It was completely different than being pregnant with Alisa. I carried Debbie differently, which made everyone suspect I was having a boy. I knew I was having another girl. With all that energy, I built a picket fence for the front yard and stained it myself. I caught trouble from the in-laws for that, too.

Debbie's birth was so different than Alisa's. She was due February 13th. She was late arriving. Sue's birthday is February 17th. I told my doctor that I was not having my child on my mother-in-law's birthday. He agreed to induce labor on the 16th if I had not gone into labor by then. This decision turned out to be for the best.

The 16th came, so James took me to the hospital. The doctor induced labor at about 6 A.M. I was in labor all morning. Around 1 P.M., the doctor came in to see how I was progressing. I was getting there, but my water had not yet broken. The doctor left, saying he would be back soon. James had been at my side unless he needed a cigarette. He went to smoke just before the doctor came back. The doctor broke my water and the shit hit the fan. Debbie's heartbeat dropped in half every time I had a contraction. The nurses had me turn on my side, then had me get on my knees. Nothing helped. I heard we have to get this baby out. I was wheeled to the operating room. I could feel my belly being swabbed. I heard the doctor's voice say, "Okay, folks, let's get this show on the road." I calmed down because I knew I was in trusted hands. Water broken at 2 P.M., baby delivered at 2:05 P.M.

James returned from his smoke as I was being wheeled down the hall. I didn't see him. We had discussed getting my tubes tied after this child. Well, the doctor came out and explained what happened. The umbilical cord was wrapped around Debbie's neck twice. Every time I pushed, I was choking her. He told James the baby was a girl and asked if he was sure that we wanted my tubes tied. James said, "If you don't do it, she'll kill me."

Since Debbie had been born through an emergency C-section, I was not allowed to carry her or go upstairs. James was allowed to work remotely from home. His office was in the basement of the house, so he took the baby monitor down there with him. If I needed anything, I would ask him to come upstairs. Many times, I would have to ask more than once for him to respond. He wasn't as excited about Debbie as he had been with Alisa.

When Debbie was born, Alisa liked having a baby sister but would get jealous when Debbie was getting all the attention. I was feeding Debbie one afternoon, and even though Alisa was potty trained, she stood next to the chair I was in and peed in the register.

In May, we decided to take Alisa to Disney World. Debbie was three months old, so she stayed with her Smith grandparents. We felt this was a way to show Alisa that she shouldn't feel any less loved because Debbie had arrived. I think the trip was only a few days, not a full week. James wanted to make the most of the trip. It was his vacation time and his money, so we were going to do things his way. Alisa wanted to be at the park when it opened, but James would sleep in. By the time he got up, Alisa was barely containing her excitement. We went to the park each day for three days, I believe. We didn't have a lot of money for food and souvenirs. We had gotten food at the grocery store with the plan that we would take a lunch break each day, not only to eat but to allow Alisa to take a nap. (Remember, she was almost three.)

The lunch break never happened. James decided that since we were spending the money, we were going to get the most out of it. We walked through the park and rode the rides that Alisa could go on, but James wanted to do the more adult rides. Alisa and I would have to wait while he went on his ride. He continued to push Alisa and me to keep going. Alisa was starving by one in the afternoon. She was crying and cranky. I did get her something small to eat to keep her going. We stayed at the park until nearly nightfall. James wanted to stay for the parade of lights and fireworks. I finally put my foot down. I had been carrying and cajoling a two-and-a-half-year-old for about three hours. He finally agreed to go back to the hotel. The minute we got on the transport to take us to our car, Alisa was asleep in my arms.

When we went to the Orlando airport for our flight home, I had quite a scare. James was ahead of Alisa and me at the airport and started up the escalator to check in. I had a hold of Alisa's hand. She let go to show me she could hang on by herself. I turned around to steady myself on the up escalator, but when I turned back around, Alisa was going down, not up. I tried to run and catch her before she got too far out of sight, but to no avail. I rushed up the escalator, trying to catch James. He is six feet, so my stride could never keep up with him. I got to the top and headed for security. I was in a panic. Security called for a missing child. While I was talking to security, James walked up and demanded to know where Alisa was. I said she had taken the down escalator to the floors below. He got angry at me for letting go of her hand. Luckily, she was found quickly and returned to us. This was the first of many times that I would be in a panic because she was out of my sight.

As Debbie grew, James kept his distance at times. When he played with her, it usually meant he was playing with both girls. Alisa loved having Debbie around. Alisa was the leader, with Debbie following along behind. She would make up stories and play with the Barbie dolls with Debbie. Alisa would always help to encourage Debbie to stand up. I have a picture in my mind of the girls standing together at the storm door, watching for Grandma and Grandpa Smith.

Debbie was a bigger baby than Alisa. She was two inches longer and one ounce heavier. Due to her long legs, her feet were bent inward, pushing on my lungs. I really did not notice the bow of her legs until she started trying to walk. She was slow to walk. When she stood up, she looked like she had been riding a horse. I was concerned that she would have to have surgery to repair her legs. The doctor told me to give it a little time; she may just need braces for a while. I was overjoyed when Debbie could finally stand and walk on her own. In one of her baby pictures, she is standing holding on the back of a chair. The bow in her legs can be seen quite clearly. I was very happy when this condition resolved itself with no medical intervention.

My dad had to have open-heart surgery in the summer of 1989. Debbie had been born in February. Mom and Dad had not yet met her. I went to New York with Debbie while Alisa stayed home with James. By wrapping Debbie in a blanket and holding her on my left side and walking on Mom's left side, we were able to sneak her into the cardiac

ICU unit. She got to meet her Grandpa Colton. He was so pleased. I like to think the visit helped him get through surgery and recover.

When I returned from New York, I found that Sue and Richard were taking care of Alisa. James had only put her to bed at night. He had spent most of the time in the basement on his computer. He had gotten a good job as a programmer after he finished technical school. He was using the computer for work and to improve his programming skills. At that time, I feel his time on the computer was split between programming and chatting with other women such as Wendy, the administrative assistant from his office.

It wasn't too long after, Wendy began calling the house and asking James to come to help her. The first couple of times I let it go, but when the calls came almost every weekend, I told James he had to tell her no, that she needed to find someone else to help her. I asked him why he wouldn't help me when I needed help. He said, "You don't need my help. You're an Amazon. You can handle anything. That is why I married you." I felt betrayed because I interpreted this to mean he was not my partner in this life. A few months later, he did say that I wasn't his best friend. His wife and best friend were two different people in his mind.

In the meantime, James started "helping" other women who needed it. He wanted to play the part of hero to every woman but me. We fought over it a lot. With two little girls to take care of, I didn't have much energy to fight with him. I was working full-time as well. I had always thought you married your best friend.

# CHAPTER FOUR
## *Florida*

James left the job where Wendy worked. I don't remember for sure, but I think he was fired for hacking the computer system. His next job was with a consulting company who wanted him to go to Florida for a three-month assignment. He agreed and left for Florida just after Christmas because he had to report to work the first working day of 1991.

The girls missed him dearly. I was trying to figure out how to be a single parent, raising the girls on my own. I guess it was just practice for later in life. The first month James was down there, he called often. My thirtieth birthday was that year. My birthday was also Super Bowl Sunday. I waited all day for him to call, but nothing. I finally called him, yelling at him. I was so upset that he forgot. He said he had been invited to a Super Bowl party and just forgot. He sent me flowers at work the next day, but it still didn't heal the hurt.

To further make up for forgetting, he asked me to come visit him. I flew down to enjoy the weekend with him. We went to see the movie *Robin Hood: Prince of Thieves.* As the movie was ending, which I felt was very romantic, James remarked something about his friend Joy would love the movie. Again, I was hurt. We went back to his apartment and went to sleep. About two in the morning, Joy called wanting to talk to James. I asked who she was, but she wouldn't tell me. Then she asked who I was, and I said, "I'm his wife." James took the phone from me and told her he would call her in a few days.

In the morning, I was making the bed and I found a pair of panties in his bed. When I confronted him, he said that he and Joy did laundry together. He explained that he had met her at the midnight showing of *The Rocky Horror Picture Show.* She worked at the theater, and they had become friends. I really did not believe him. I flew home and tried to put it out of my mind.

The three-month contract was extended to a year, so James came back to Ohio, and we moved to Florida with him. It was a hard transition for me. I wasn't going to get a job. I knew no one and only had the girls for company. When James would come home, it was a guessing game as to what mood he was in.

Florida is a different world. I had grown up with the mindset of getting your chores done first, then go play. In Florida, I had to turn that around because it got so hot in the afternoon. I would take the girls to the pool or let them ride their bikes around the apartment complex. Debbie learned to swim while we were in Florida. James and I would stand a few feet apart and encourage Debbie to swim to the other, like we did when she was learning to walk. This was, I think, the only plus that came from us going to Florida.

Those afternoons, while the girls were out playing, I took up sewing again. I made a real simple quilt out of squares. Alisa loved it. I made her another quilt a few years later, which disappeared over time, but this one she always kept. It was in her car a lot. I have several pictures of my twenty-something daughter asleep in her bed covered by that simple, and by then worn-out, quilt. I felt she kept that one because it made her feel close to me. We would exchange the "I love you" pretty often but the blanket was always there for her.

The girls played with kids from the complex almost every day. One day, Alisa accidentally stepped on a lizard. She was horrified that she killed something. To make it worse, the other kids started calling her a lizard killer. She came in crying. I feel having killed the lizard, she felt like a bad person. It took her a while to calm down.

Another adjustment the girls and I had to accept when we got to Florida was James had gotten a dog. A German Shepherd even. He knew I was terrified of shepherds because a friend of mine had been attacked by one when we were young. Her whole face was stitches—I don't know how many, but it was a lot. James had named the dog Izzy. The girls took an immediate like to him, but I had to take it a baby step at a time.

Florida was full of bugs. I went into the bathroom one morning, and there was a huge palmetto bug on the back of the toilet. I screamed, and James came running. Then he just laughed and said I had to get used to them. He dismissed my fear as just get over it. I was hurt that my feelings of fear, regardless of how minor, were just brushed off.

James continued to go to movies on Saturday. He insisted Joy was just a friend. She continued to call the apartment to talk to him. I would insist that he tell her that they could not be friends, but he ignored me, just as he had with Wendy. We fought a lot about this, along with our differences in parenting styles. The stress of the situation and the rejection from James pushed me to my limit.

I finally had it and left Florida. I drove back to Ohio with my two little girls. The girls and I had been in Florida for about three months. Back then, car seats weren't as secure as they are now. I remember stopping for gas. When I had finished pumping, I locked the car doors and went to pay. When I came out, Debbie was standing at the steering wheel and had peed on the driver's seat. It was a long drive from Georgia to Ohio.

Once we got back and settled into our house, James started calling to apologize. At first, I was stern with him and said he made his choice and had to live with it. I did not want to be a single parent, and the girls always wanted to talk to him. He finally wore me down. When the assignment was over, he returned home crying because he wanted his family back.

James moved his computer from the basement into the corner of the dining room. He was on that machine constantly. He was addicted to chat rooms. He was always chatting with some woman or another. The girls would ask him to play with them, and he would say in a minute, but the minute never came. He was physically in the house but not present.

One evening, his monitor went out. He started yelling at me that he had to go buy another one immediately. I said we had no money for one. We did not have any credit cards at that time either. He stayed angry and depressed until I figured out a way to get the money for a new one. Our car was paid off, so I was able to get a loan using the car as collateral. He finally calmed down and came out of his depression. As I look back on it now, it was the equivalent of giving a drug addict their next fix. I was the devoted wife who wanted him to be happy.

The bouts of James' depression started getting longer and longer. At first, it was a couple of days. Then a week or more. I teased him by saying that he had PMS, not me. His depression got to the point where he was more depressed than happy. I began to feel like I was walking on eggshells. The manic side of his bipolar disorder played out with his lack of need for sleep. He would be up until 2 or 3 A.M. The following day would be full of his angry outbursts.

We spent about six months or so in our Ohio house after returning from Florida. During that time, we saw James' parents often. They bought the girls a swing set that we put up in the backyard. Money was still tight, like it always was. Alisa asked for a toy once, and I told her no, that we didn't have the money. She looked at me and said, "That's okay. Grandma will buy it for me." I knew then that we had to move away from the in-laws.

The grandparents doted on the girls. They rarely said no to anything the girls wanted. They took them to the petting zoo, always shopping and trick-or-treating on Halloween. They would buy the girls new expensive dresses for the holidays. Once we moved away, the doting settled down a bit, which was a plus.

After moving away, Sue and Richard would send multiple boxes of gifts for Christmas. The girls would get boxes from Great Aunt Sue and Uncle Walt. Walt was Richard's brother. Sue E. (as she was known to keep the two Sues straight) and Walt considered Alisa and Debbie almost like their own grandchildren.

# CHAPTER FIVE
## *Maryland*

James' next contract was in the D.C. area. I did not want to live in the D.C. area, but we were still trying to work on our marriage. We all moved to Gaithersburg, Maryland.

I stopped watching the news during this time because every night it was about how many people got killed and how many burglaries happened. It scared me to live there. I started looking for a job and had an interview in downtown D.C. I was terrified to go down there. James said it would be okay unless I got caught in rush-hour traffic. I had asked the neighbor lady to watch the girls. I told her that I should be back in a couple of hours.

Lo and behold, I got lost getting to the interview. I had missed the appointment, so I decided to just turn around and go home. I was soon to learn that in D.C., a street could be two lanes or one way in the morning but then become a one-way going the opposite direction during afternoon rush hour. I could not go back the way I came. It took me three hours to get home. I had never been in traffic like that before. It was raining and I was crying. I was worried about the babysitter and how she would react. It was before cellphones, so I could not call to tell her that I was lost. When I finally arrived back to the sitter's house, I was a terrified mess. She proceeded to yell at me that I was inconsiderate for being late. I tried to apologize, but she shut the door in my face. That was a really bad day for me. I told James when he got home. He just blew me off and asked what was for dinner.

I finally got a job working second shift from 5:30 P.M. to 1 A.M. in a D.C. suburb. We started looking for part-time daycare only to find out that Alisa was old enough to go to school in Maryland. She had not been old enough in Ohio until the following year. I took her and got her registered for school, and she started the next day. I put her on the school bus in the morning and waited at the bus stop for her return. The bus arrived and I watched as all the kids get off the bus, but no Alisa. I tried to stop the bus driver to ask where Alisa was, but she shut the door and drove off. I was in such a panic. This was another one of those times that I was terrified because she was out of sight.

I called the school. They said that she had gotten on the bus. Someone went to check the bus since it had just arrived back at school. Alisa was there, all curled up on a seat, sleeping. The school called, and I went to pick her up. After that, Alisa always got off the bus. I decided that the girls would not ride a bus to any school unless absolutely necessary.

I started the job working second shift. James got home around 6 in the afternoon, so the girls only needed a babysitter for a couple of hours each day. We found someone, a nice lady, in the apartment complex. The situation seemed pretty good because they would be with one parent or another most of the time. Two hours a day was not long for them to be at a babysitter.

The situation was working fine until I found out from a neighbor that James was leaving the girls home alone sometimes at night. Debbie was three, and Alisa was five. If James had forgotten cigarettes or Pepsi, he would go to the store and leave these two innocent little girls alone.

I found out about the abandonment of the girls on a weekend when James had decided to go back to Ohio "to see his parents." I knew that was not why he was going, but didn't say anything. With him gone for the weekend, I could relax a little bit. The neighbor across the parking lot came over, and we were chatting when he told me about James leaving the girls alone. He said he had been tempted to call Social Services. I am glad he didn't. I now had a new worry. Did James leave the kids alone while I was working tonight?

Relaxation did not come that weekend as I had hoped. The girls were out front playing, and I was in the house on the phone with my mom. Alisa suddenly burst through the door, yelling that Debbie was bleeding. I slammed the phone down on my mom. By the time I got to the door, Debbie was on the steps just outside the door. I yelled at Alisa to get some wet washcloths so I could clean Debbie up.

I got Debbie inside and onto the couch, lying down. I took the washcloths to Debbie's face, wiping the blood off. She was covered in it. As the blood started to clot and I removed more of it from her, I could see her jawbone. She had fallen face-first onto a concrete step and hit her chin. I knew this was more than just "kiss the booboo and make it all better." After getting both girls in the car, with Debbie holding a washcloth to her face, we headed for the closest urgent care.

We arrived, and I carried Debbie inside with Alisa in tow. The doctor said that Debbie needed stitches. She was crying and twisting her head, so they wrapped her in a papoose-like contraption to keep her still. I was standing there on Debbie's left side. Alisa went around to Debbie's right side and held her hand, talking to her to calm her down. The doctor looked at me and told me to leave the room because of how pale I had become. He said he didn't need two patients.

The doctor put two stitches in Debbie's chin. Alisa never left her side. She just kept talking to her to keep her calm. I was amazed and thankful that she could do that. I took them home. Debbie lay on the couch, and Alisa tried to keep her entertained to keep her mind off the pain. I tried to call James but could not reach him. When he returned from the trip, he cuddled Debbie a little, then went to the basement and went back on the computer. I took her to get the stitches out. Debbie was nervous, but she handled it well. Alisa stayed at home with James.

# CHAPTER SIX

## *Colorado (1992-1996)*

In late summer, the contract James was on was coming to an end, so James started looking for another job to stay in D.C. He was offered a job with MCI, with the stipulation that he would have to relocate to Colorado. Without consulting me, he jumped at the chance and asked, "Where do I sign?" Even though he had not consulted me, this was one step I was excited about. I hated Maryland and couldn't wait to go West. It also meant that we did not have to go back to Ohio and be around James' parents again. This was 1992.

MCI paid to fly us to Colorado Springs for two weeks to find housing. We explored the city, where MCI was opening its new headquarters. I thought I was in Heaven. It just felt like home. It was hard to find housing because the market was so hot with MCI moving many more in. Colorado Springs is a military town, so there is always movement of troops in and out. We finally found a house and secured it with a move-in date of September 1st.

We flew back to Maryland to settle things there. We were moved by Global Van Lines. They came in, packed us up, and even put our cars in the truck. As soon as the truck was loaded, we headed for the airport.

We had to take Izzy with us. The girls were upset that Izzy was going to be in a kennel in the belly of the plane and could not ride in the cabin with us. Izzy was given a sedative and survived just fine.

MCI had arranged for us to stay in corporate housing until our things arrived. We had five days in corporate housing, but the truck took six days to arrive. We were lucky that the house was empty, and we had gotten the keys. With the truck coming the next day, we spent that last night in an empty house. The neighbors came by and offered us cots and sleeping bags for our sleeping comfort. The next morning, they brought coffee. In all the places I had lived previously, I had never had any neighbor come and introduce themselves, much less bring us bedding and coffee.

James worked hard at MCI. The company gave him an American Express card, which became a problem in our marriage. To keep the bills paid, James had a $50.00-a-week budget to buy gas, cigarettes, and lunch. Back in the early 1990s, this was plenty. James would never pack lunch. He got in the habit of taking several coworkers out to lunch at least once a week and charging it on his American Express card. Since I oversaw paying the bills, I had a budget made out and tried hard to stick to it. We started getting American Express bills for $300 or more each month because of James' generosity. I would yell at him, but that didn't help. How were we supposed to keep food on the table when he was recklessly spending money we didn't have?

We lived in the same rental house for four years. I got a job working at Metropolitan Life, processing Medicare claims. This job was in South Denver, so I drove an hour each way to go to work. On the first day of work, I met Joan. We were in a training class together. Joan would become my best friend. She was a year or so older than I, but we got along very well. She was in customer service, and I was in claims. Working in different areas, we would have lunch together a couple times a week. She was married to Dean and had a daughter, Shari. A couple of years into our friendship, Joan got pregnant. She gave birth to a son, Toby, whom the girls adored. I looked to Joan often for support. She could make me smile.

School had started so we enrolled Alisa in the first grade. She was a bright student and loved to learn. She went to daycare before and after school. Life in the Springs seemed good for the girls. James and I would become further and further apart as his bipolar disorder became more prevalent.

Debbie was not old enough to go to school, so she went to the daycare center. I would drop the girls off. Debbie would stay at daycare all day. The daycare made sure Alisa got on and off the bus each day. Debbie started school in the fall of 1994. Adding a note here, I picked the girls up from daycare unless it was a school night. I was always there for pick up by 5:10 P.M. If I had gotten stuck in traffic, causing me to be late, the girls would get anxious and upset.

Alisa started to get more creative during this time. She would sketch pictures of different things. She read a lot. She would make up songs that she and Debbie would sing for James and me. One time, she wrote a song about Izzy and how much the girls loved him. She also started getting reckless and was easily influenced by the neighbor kids. She rode her bike into the back of a U-Haul truck that was parked across the street. She scraped her knee but wasn't hurt too bad. I asked how she had run into the truck. She said she didn't see it. How do you not see a truck? She began climbing trees and wandering past her allowed boundaries.

Both girls wanted to start gymnastics. I enrolled them in a class, and we began their weekly workouts. Girl Scouts was another activity that Alisa was interested in. She joined Brownies. I was glad for her participation in scouting. I had been a Girl Scout myself. I was in as a Brownie, Junior, and Senior. I learned a lot of life skills. I felt part of something with many friends. I wanted the girls to experience the same thing. Debbie wasn't old enough yet.

That first Christmas in Colorado came. We took the girls to see the zoo lights at the Cheyenne Mountain Zoo. It is the only zoo in the country built on the side of a mountain. We fed the giraffes face to face and walked around looking at all the displays. The evening was cold. I felt joyful seeing the smiles on the girls' faces. They were goofy little snow bunnies. Christmas itself was joyful and quiet.

Debbie's first birthday party in Colorado was amazing. Having come from Ohio and been born in February, it was quite the treat to have her birthday party mostly outside. Her friends played on the swings, and the temperature was in the 60s. Izzy enjoyed chasing the girls around. We had a simple party with cake and ice cream. I was happy.

We wanted the girls to get out as much as possible. I would suggest an outing for the weekend, and James would agree. I would tell the girls about what we had planned. They would get all excited just to have their hopes dashed come Saturday because Daddy wouldn't get up. He had stayed up most of the night on the computer doing whatever. We would wait for him, but by the time he got around, it was 1 or 2 in the afternoon. It was always such a disappointment to the girls that I started taking the girls out without him. It was better that way.

James and I had never discussed our religious beliefs prior to getting married. I had been raised in church, and although I had not gone since high school, I am strong in my belief. I wanted to have the girls baptized, but James did not. He claimed to be an agnostic. It was my turn to do something without James knowing. I took the girls to church and discussed the baptisms with the minister. He agreed, and we set a date. I told James when I got home. He made it known that he was unhappy that I went behind his back. Too bad. I didn't care. I told him what Sunday the baptisms would take place. Surprisingly enough, he showed up and participated in the event.

Watching my marriage fall apart and James' bipolar disorder getting worse, I decided I had to go back to school and finish my bachelor's degree. The writing was on the wall, and I knew I would have to provide for my family on my own, so I started school at Colorado Technical University for computer science in the spring semester of 1993. It took me nineteen years and four colleges to finish, but I finally got my degree.

After attending college for a couple of years, I was able to land a job working in IT instead of being a claims processor. The job was in Pueblo, so I started driving south for an hour every day instead of north. The job came with a $10,000 raise. I was excited to finally get my foot in the door of an IT shop. After I got the phone call that I had been hired, I ran to the basement happily to inform James, but was extremely disappointed when he said, "I didn't think you could do it."

The team I worked with was not very big. I got a lot of support from them. They taught me what it was really like to work in a real live IT shop. I learned that in IT, you don't have to punch a clock, so to speak. It took a while to get used to being able to come in a little late due to traffic and not get written up. I worked at the job for a little more than a year. Rumors started to fly about the company being sold to a California company. I was tired of driving long distances. I was able to find a job in Colorado Springs.

The job in the Springs was downtown. It was not far from the college. I stayed devoted to going to school. I normally took two classes at a time. One semester, I took three. I had an hour for lunch, so my employer allowed me to take a class during my lunch hour. If I got back late, I would stay late.

It had been mainly my responsibility for the girls. I would pick them up from daycare, take them home, make sure they did their homework, and make dinner. While I was attending school, on school nights, James would pick up the girls. Depending on his mood, I would get home to dishes done, girls in bed, and peace. Most nights, I came home to dirty dishes and James sitting on his computer in the basement while the girls were running around or fighting. James would either acknowledge my return or he would belittle me and then ignore me. I was on a roller coaster going nowhere. After working eight hours, going straight from work to class, and getting home after 8 o'clock, I hated the nights I came home to the "bad" nights. After getting everything calmed down, I had to do homework.

James started to have longer bouts of depression. Needing little sleep, he would stay up late and go to chat rooms for company. His online time got longer, and his time as a father and husband diminished. I think about it now and realize I wasn't really missing anything when James would stay in the basement. We had never been physically close, so it was better that he was out of sight. However, I was determined to keep the marriage together for two reasons. I did not want to be a single parent, and I did not want to take the girls away from their father.

The last family vacation we took was to the Grand Canyon in March of '94. It was a very scary drive down over Wolf Creek Pass into Durango. It had snowed earlier. We were driving after dark, and all I could see was the white line on the side of the highway. Conditions were windy, and the road was snow-packed and icy. I prayed the whole way through the pass. James was driving, and at times, he would scare me to death.

The trip was just for a weekend. We spent the night in Durango. We arrived late at night and went immediately to bed. The next day, we stopped at the Four Corners for pictures. This is the only place in the United States where you can stand in four states all at the same time: Colorado, New Mexico, Arizona, and Utah. The experience was kind of cool.

We arrived at the canyon in the early afternoon. The canyon has many lookout points with railings around them for visitors to get close to the edge without falling off a cliff. James was afraid of heights. As we explored that afternoon, James was constantly yelling for the girls to get away from the edge. If they got within twenty feet of the edge, he would yell. I was very upset that we could not enjoy the canyon.

The following morning, there was a cloud hanging in the canyon. It was so beautiful and peaceful. I felt we could walk across it. The girls and I were in awe. I know James was there, but I don't remember him being with us. He was probably off smoking a cigarette. It was a quiet and peaceful moment that I enjoyed with my girls.

Later that summer, I had vacation time and wanted to take the girls to see my family. James had time off as well. I asked him to go, and he declined. It was just as well. The three of us had a good time at my mother's house. We went to a family picnic over to my brother Tim's in-laws' pond. Many of the family came. I can still see Tim at the grill when he turned and asked where my "good for nothing" husband was. I just shrugged my shoulders. I had a video camera, so I went back to filming the kids either in the pond or near it. There was a kiddie pool for the youngest of the bunch.

When we returned from NY, James had a letter for me. It asked why couldn't I understand that he was void of all feeling. He had stayed in his pajamas the entire ten days we were gone. He had not showered or shaved. He had spent the entire time chatting (or whatever) on his computer. When I asked about seeking counseling, he said he knew he had a problem, but he could handle it. I decided it was time to start thinking about a divorce.

During all the online chatting, James had met a woman by the name of Donna, but people called her DJ. She lived up in the mountains with her two children. She eventually moved to Denver. After separating, James spent a lot of time in Denver. During one of the many fights we had, he told me he had no friends because I was always a bitch to people who called for him. He then went on telling me how DJ thought he was a good guy.

Those thoughts about divorce included how James would discipline Alisa and, by that time, ignore Debbie. He was heavy-handed with Alisa when he did decide to step in. He was also intense with the birthday spankings. It wasn't just a slight tap on the butt. It was almost like he was punishing her and Debbie for being born. He would laugh while doing it, but I could hear the sting when his hand hit its mark.

Alisa was really upset and yelling one day, over what, I don't remember. James spanked her so hard and long that I felt I had to step in to stop him. Alisa slammed her bedroom door. James was still yelling at her to open the door. She refused because of how hard he had hit her. James got his tools and took the door off. Alisa was eight at the time.

We spent time discussing our parenting styles. I believed in discipline, but not to excess. We would ground the girls at times. Video games were becoming popular, and we decided we were not going to indulge the girls by getting one. However, that last Christmas, James went behind my back and bought the girls a video game set (Nintendo, I think). I was extremely angry with him, but did not show it so the girls would not feel bad. I started feeling like I had three children instead of a husband and two children. I think he started looking at me like I was his mother.

We made it through Christmas for the girls' sake, but in January, I met with a lawyer to draw up divorce papers. I filed with the court on February 14th. He was served shortly after. James did not hire a lawyer during the divorce. We met with my lawyer and came up with an agreement. When we met with her, she told him that he had to leave the house, or we could take legal action.

I expected James to move out. He did not. He stayed in the basement, which was just a family room, bathroom, and laundry room. He slept on the couch downstairs. I kept telling him to find a place to live. His reply was always "I can't afford an apartment." When he finally did move out, he took Izzy with him. This broke the girls' hearts, especially Alisa's, because Izzy slept at the end of her bed at night. She asked who was going to protect her now that Izzy was gone. She was more upset that the dog was gone than she was about her father.

In the divorce agreement, which was to be finalized in the fall, James was granted parenting time every other weekend. These visits became a sore spot for me. James was dating DJ (and others), and the girls had to meet every one of them. He would pick the girls up Saturday morning.

Then he would have whoever he was seeing, at the moment, come over for dinner. He would leave the girls in the living room to watch movies or play video games while he and his latest fling went into the bedroom. He would return the girls on Sunday afternoon.

I tried to discuss the moral issue behind his behavior and point out what kind of example he was setting. His response was, "My parenting time should not be spent just watching them sleep." He would show the girls off and use them to meet new women. When he started getting more involved with DJ, he would leave the girls with a babysitter. He would drive to Denver, spend the night at her house, and come back the next morning.

Many times, the girls told me that Daddy spent a lot of Sunday mornings sleeping. They were not getting quality time with Dad, but they were being exposed to immoral behavior. I felt they were being used as pawns by him to show other women that he was a good man. I felt I had another decision to make.

The court date for the divorce was Alisa's 9th birthday, October 3rd. She never knew we were in court on that day because the papers weren't finalized until October 17, 1995. He was ordered to pay child support and one-half of the unpaid medical bills. The visitation rights were upheld, with Thanksgiving and Christmas being alternated.

After the divorce, my parenting style changed. I was devoted to the girls. I let guilt guide me in how to parent my children. I felt that I had taken them away from their father, so I had to fill the void by being both mother and father to them.

Having grown up in a very small town with few activities for kids, I wanted the girls to have access to any activity they wanted to try. I was very naïve when I left to go to college. I did not want the girls to experience the same embarrassment that I had when I moved to the city. I allowed them to try almost anything they showed interest in.

I made the decision not to remarry because of all the stories of new husbands abusing stepdaughters. I only had the girls for a few years while I had another thirty to forty years. I was not going to miss a single moment of their lives if I could help it. I dated a few times, but I never introduced any of the men to the girls. It was none of their business. James would tell me to get out and have some fun, leave the girls at daycare, and have a drink. He did not understand that I was the girls' stability.

During these four years in Colorado Springs, I began to get depressed. I loved Colorado, but it just wasn't enough at the time. I started feeling like I wasn't attractive. I felt rejection, hurt, and anger. I had to keep those feelings buried much of the time for the girls' sake. For my own sanity, I started going to counseling. I went weekly. She prescribed Xanax for depression. As I tried to work through divorce issues as well as abuse issues, my counselor kept asking about my support system. What was that? I hadn't had one since my college days. I said my sister Paula was asking me to move to Missouri. She said she would help me raise the girls. My counselor asked what I was waiting for. That decision was made.

Colorado law, at that time, specified that if a custodial parent was moving, the non-custodial parent had to be given notice. I don't remember what the timeframe was, but it was a short time, maybe a day or two. I started packing, and with Joan's help, we got almost everything packed and into the garage. James had visitation the weekend before we were to move, so we only packed what was not obvious until after he returned the girls on Sunday. I quickly finished packing. I told James the day before the move. The movers showed up and started loading. Shortly after, James showed up and made a scene, saying I couldn't take his children out of state. He would file kidnapping charges against me. I explained the law to him and indicated that I had obeyed the divorce law in Colorado, and I was leaving. Alisa climbed a tree in the front yard and started yelling at James. Debbie stood on the other side of the lawn and cried.

The decision to leave was a good one. James was going to make good on his threat to hunt me down. I was no longer afraid of him physically, but I was certainly afraid that he was never going to leave me alone. The emotional abuse would continue for many years.

# CHAPTER SEVEN

## *Preteen in Missouri*

The move to Missouri was a good place to start over for me. Having divorced James and moved away, we all seemed happier. We moved into a rented condo in Lake St. Louis. This area is known for expensive houses. Some people had boats to use on the lake, and most wore name-brand clothes.

During that first year, the girls got to start over as well. New schools, new friends, and new activities. I went to enroll them in school, only to find out that Missouri required an additional vaccination than Colorado. We went to the clinic and the girls got their shots.

It was Valentine's Day. Debbie was very upset that she had to start school on the day she had her shot. She was more upset that she would not know anyone and would feel left out of the Valentine exchange. The teacher got her involved quickly by having her help another girl get ready for their party. Debbie ended up getting a few handmade Valentines. Alisa, on the other hand, just went with the flow. She went to her classroom and started making friends and catching on to the work. At the end of the day, Alisa said that the new school curriculum was just going over things that she had learned in Colorado.

Valentine's Day was tough for me. It still is. I have only ever gotten one gift on Valentine's Day. I got a promise ring in 1980. Knowing how the day always felt to me, I wanted to make sure the girls always knew they were loved. I would buy the girls a card and chocolate, or sometimes a stuffed animal with a balloon. One Valentine's Day, I purchased stuffed animals. I don't remember Debbie's, but I do remember Alisa's. It was a gray bear with red ears and a red bow. She named it Mr. Fuzzykins. She slept with it a lot.

Wentzville was small compared to the surrounding cities. It is about seven miles from Lake St. Louis and was more affordable. I felt safe in Wentzville, so I decided to have a house built there. We all needed stability, which the house would help us achieve. Each of the girls got to choose the carpet color for their rooms. Debbie chose blue and Alisa chose purple. The house wasn't big and expensive. It was about 1300 square feet with three bedrooms. We had a good-sized yard that I had to landscape. (I have a brown thumb.) We would go over about twice a week to check on the progress. The build took about four months. It was exciting to see.

During our stay in the condo, we had a couple of men living next door, and one of them would help me when I needed it. His name was Greg. As we were unpacking and putting the boxes in the garage, Greg helped the girls make a fort out of the boxes. Greg soon became a substitute father to the girls. He would come over in the evenings sometimes, and we would all play games. One night, we were playing UNO. Greg said something that we all thought was hilarious. We burst out laughing. Alisa had a mouth full of orange juice, which she spat everywhere, but mostly on Greg. Greg laughed it off and started to play like he was going after her. It was fun to relax and enjoy simple things without worrying about the backlash that would have come if it had been James and not Greg. We had a good time that night.

Greg and I had a four-year affair. I was beaten down from being married to James, and I needed to know that I was still desirable to someone. He was married, but I did not know that when we began to get involved. I just knew that I needed what he was offering. His wife lived in Arkansas. He would return to Arkansas the first weekend of every month for his Army Reserve obligation. He was in Missouri for his job with GTE. His position moved to Missouri. His wife's position was scheduled to move later. Greg just never talked about his family.

I went to work at Edward Jones Investments, so I needed before-and after-school care. I have to say that God had a hand in helping me find a sitter. Her name was Pat. She had placed an ad in the local weekly paper, to which I responded. Our meeting was meant to be. We hit it off right away and are still friends. She is a wonderful person whose life was kid-focused. She had quiet time for the kids to do homework or read. She limited the amount of time that the girls could watch television. She even let them finger paint on her counter. During the summer, she would take them on adventures occasionally. These adventures were nothing elaborate, but they were bonding experiences that I feel were very beneficial to the girls, who were just beginning to develop trust again. I couldn't have found a better person.

I went back to college. I went to school nights and weekends at Maryville University. It seemed odd to me that I was going to graduate from the same college as my sister Paula. Paula and I had gone in completely different directions. She had gone into the Air Force and was stationed in Illinois. She eventually ended up in the St. Louis area by

1984, about three months before James and I got married. I had gone to Indiana, then to Columbus, Ohio, where I met and married James.

The nights I had school, the girls were taken care of by a friend of Paula's named Sara. She was excellent with the girls. She made the girls do their homework. It was refreshing to have someone I could depend on, unlike the uncertainty of how James handled them. Sara was kind but firm and a good cook. She would make enough dinner so that the leftovers would be in the fridge when I got home.

It was during the time in the condo that Alisa began to change. She had always been outspoken and creative, but now she started being reckless as well. She started taking unnecessary risks without any thought of the consequences. I caught her climbing out of her bedroom window onto the sloped porch roof. She started to climb the trees on the condo grounds. During one of the tree-climbing episodes, Joe (her cousin) was with her. Joe fell out of the tree. He fractured two vertebrae and had to wear a brace for two months. He missed the year-end trip that was part of the fourth-grade experience. Joe could not participate in many of the activities at camp. Paula was furious. Paula did not tell me at the time (or I forgot), but I understand now and would have been furious too.

We had other kids on the street for the girls to play with, so many days in the summer, the girls would be "down the street" playing. One afternoon, Debbie came running home yelling, "Mom, Alisa's hurt. She can't breathe. She fell off the trampoline." I went rushing down and found Alisa lying on the ground. She was breathing and basically fine. I concluded that she just had the wind knocked out of her. I made her come home.

Alisa started having bursts of anger for no reason. One afternoon, we got home after a day of school and work. We walked in the door, and

Alisa dropped her backpack on the floor. We had a coat rack that the girls were supposed to hang their backpacks on so they could always find them. I asked Alisa to please pick the backpack up and put it on the hook. She flew into a rage, yelling at me, telling me that I had ruined her whole day. She did pick the bag up and hung it up, but she continued to scream and yell. I went about the house doing normal things to try to let her de-escalate— changing my clothes, starting dinner, and starting laundry. Alisa followed me everywhere, screaming at me. She even followed me to the basement when I put the clothes in the washer. My mind remembers some kind of dark event happening in the basement, but I cannot bring it into focus. Alisa may have threatened me.

The living room of the condo had a loft/balcony structure. It wasn't very wide. It was a place where the girls could play with whoever was in the living room. That day, as Alisa was having her outburst, she went up there and continued expressing her anger. She wasn't screaming anymore, but because she was above the room, her voice boomed into the living room. It took most of that night to get her calmed down. As I lay in bed that night, my mind was wondering if this is what a teenager acted like. She was nine then. How much worse was it going to be? I know I hadn't been that way when I was a teenager, but having older siblings, I could remember some outbursts around our house among the boys. I decided to let it ride. From then on, I would lie in bed every night and rethink the day. What went right, what went wrong, but most importantly, what had I taught my children that day? This reflection, every night before sleep, I found to be a very useful tool. I could see where I had gotten caught up in the drama without looking at what was really going on.

We moved into the new house in May of 1997 and spent the summer settling in. The girls were quick to make friends with the neighbor kids. The kids were mostly boys with three or four girls in the mix. Alisa was always trying to prove something to the boys. Her bedroom window was over the concrete patio. She started hanging out the window without thinking about the consequences. Again, I questioned if this was normal teenage behavior, so I put a quick end to it.

James had been livid with me when we moved to Missouri. While we lived in the condo, James was still angry, but he was involved with DJ, so that kept his mind occupied. He would call the girls and talk. When Debbie told him we were having a house built, he lost control. He screamed at her with "I'm not sending child support for her to build a house for her to retire in." The thought that the house was for the girls did not even enter his brain. All hell broke loose until I agreed to meet with his attorney.

James had hired a lawyer for post-divorce issues. He made outrageous demands, such as I would pay for plane tickets for the girls every other week, so he could have his parenting time. He wanted itemized receipts for every time I took either daughter to the doctors. He wanted summer visitation and every holiday (Thanksgiving and Christmas). I thought he had lost his mind. He would call and yell at me over stupid things.

I flew to Colorado in July to address these post-divorce demands. The girls were already in Colorado for their summer visit. I was not allowed to see them as it was James' time.

We met at the lawyer's office. The lawyer had to keep James under control. James continued his outrageous demands, but the lawyer was able to make him see reason within Colorado laws. We settled on trading Thanksgiving and Christmas. James got six weeks in the summer, which

I had to pay the plane tickets for. He still had to pay child support and half of the unpaid medical bills. As it turned out, he only paid child support when he was working and never paid his half of the medical bills.

For the medical bills, he wanted me to produce an itemized bill with a copy of the check I had written as proof of services and payment. Most times, the payment was made with a credit card. I did not have time to go through all that, and besides, after insurance paid, and I paid it was nearly impossible to get itemized statements. I never understood (nor do I now) how the State of Colorado would let him get away without paying his portion as outlined in the divorce agreement. The fact that he could get out of paying half of the unpaid medical bills became a big issue as time went on.

I could not afford to stay in a hotel while I was in Colorado, going over James' demands. Joan allowed me to stay in her spare bedroom. The mattress sagged in the middle. I stayed two nights. I returned home to having back issues. The pain would begin in my lower back and proceed down my left leg. I returned to work trying to deal with the pain. By Friday, I was in so much pain that I left work early. I could barely drive home. I had no feeling in my foot. I was able to drive since it was my left leg, but the pain in my back was excruciating.

I got home and went straight to bed. I had a waterbed. Not a good thing for a bad back. The heat from the bed felt good. I got the heating pad out and lay on it. I fell asleep. The next morning, I could barely move. I could not get out of bed at all. I had a house phone on the nightstand next to me. I called Paula. She drove over and came in to help me. I had given her a house key when we moved in, just for situations like this. She called nearly every chiropractor in St. Charles County, trying to find one that had Saturday hours. She was successful in finding one. However, he only had office hours until noon, and it was around 11. She convinced him to stay open and take me as a patient. She drove me there to receive my first adjustment.

The treatment was to get an adjustment every day for a certain number of days and then gradually taper off. I was told to get rid of the waterbed. At home, I had to lie flat on the floor with a rolled-up towel under my knees. I was to use an alternate of ice for twenty minutes and then twenty minutes with no ice. My back pain continued for several weeks. I did not go back to work for a while.

James was scheduled to send the girls home while I was still unable to walk. I had to be at their arrival gate to pick them up. No one else was allowed to do it. It had to be me. Greg agreed to drive me to the airport. He got a wheelchair and pushed me to the gate. (This was before 9-11, so there weren't the security issues that we have today.) Needless to say, the girls were very upset seeing me in the wheelchair. Once we got home, they were so supportive. They waited on me. I liked being waited on. It was a nice change. I still have back issues to this day.

I liked working for Edward Jones because the projects I was assigned to were designed to help the representatives in the field. However, I did not like being so far from home. The commute was around 25 miles and included crossing a bridge. Most days, the drive took about 45 minutes. However, if there were any traffic issues, the drive could become one and a half to two hours easily. Each route to work had a bridge to cross. Traffic would always slow down when a bridge was close.

During this time, I finally got a cellphone. If I got stuck in traffic, I could call the girls and let them know. Having it also allowed them to call me if they had any problems. It was a double-edged sword. If the girls were fighting, the one being treated the worst would call me. My anxiety level increased dramatically on those days. It was usually Debbie who called. Alisa's mood swings were the cause of the calls.

A tornado went by the house while the girls were home alone after school. I was stuck on the bridge in a traffic jam. Alisa called and asked what to do. I told her to take Debbie and Holly (the dog) and go to the basement. I told her to stay as far away from windows as they could get. I told them to take one of their mattresses to the basement and hide behind it. I was terrified while I sat helpless in traffic. A good quality of Alisa's was her ability to stay calm during a crisis. She had displayed it when Debbie cut her chin open and showed it on this day as well. I admired her strength. Sara arrived a short time later and called to say they were all fine.

# CHAPTER EIGHT

## *Preteen in Missouri Continues*

Alisa wanted to be a cheerleader. Cheerleaders were for high school sports, but Alisa was only in middle school. I found that she could be a cheerleader for the Wentzville little league football team. She would practice every day. The cheer team met twice a week, I believe. I remember going to football games in the cold. One game, I remember, was in the rain. The cheerleaders had to perform at halftime. They had learned a dance routine that was choreographed to the song "Celebration" by Kool and the Gang. In the pouring rain, these girls were in the middle of a field dancing. Every time I hear that song, I see my baby out on the field dancing her heart out.

Alisa took up playing the trumpet and singing in the choir. She started journaling and drawing. She was a pretty good doodler. The tattoo that I have on my right shoulder is her artwork with her signature. Some of her later drawings were very good, but with a dark undertone. Debbie joined the choir in elementary school. Later on, Debbie wanted to take art lessons. There was a local artist who gave lessons. I enrolled Debbie there.

Both girls like to read. Alisa more than Debbie during this time. She had her nose in a book quite often. However, as the bipolar disorder started emerging, Alisa was too restless to read. She started sleeping less as well.

Debbie and Alisa both liked to be athletic, so I enrolled them in gymnastics. Alisa was pretty flexible and was proud when she accomplished a new feat. Debbie tried hard and enjoyed the class. Debbie liked to laugh at her falls, then she would try again. The organization gave ribbons to all the kids as they completed harder moves. The school had a parents' night, where we could go and watch what the kids were learning and, if brave enough, try some feats of our own. I took the video camera and filmed some of each girl. While I was filming, Alisa tried the uneven parallel bars; she fell and got up laughing, telling me I needed to send the video to *America's Funniest Home Videos.*

One Christmas season, the girls had to perform on the same night, Debbie with the choir and Alisa with the band. It was a hectic night because I had to be in two places at once. The girls had to perform in two different locations, about five miles apart. Debbie's performance started first at the local hospital, so I dropped her off, then raced to the school and dropped Alisa off. I raced back to the hospital to pick up Debbie, then back to the school to see the end of the band performance. I did not get to watch Debbie's performance at all. I did get to see maybe twenty minutes of the band concert. I felt sad that I had missed out on Debbie's performance.

I remember James coming to Wentzville just once while we lived there. He came for a performance Debbie was involved in. I took him back to the airport the following day. During that ride, I made a positive decision that helped me put the past behind me. I told him that I forgave him for what he had done to me. I was far from over it, but I took the first step in healing.

Alisa started paying attention to fashion and would ask for clothes that I couldn't afford. She got a job babysitting for a couple of kids after school. Much of her money went for shoes and jewelry. She had to have her "bling" on. Sometime during our Wentzville years, Alisa also started working at the gymnastics school, where she had been a student.

The dark times in Wentzville became more routine as Alisa's behavior changed with her condition. I did not know what it was yet, but I felt like she was a firecracker waiting to go off, like her father had been at the end of our marriage. She would go to school with a smile. She had this belief that when she walked into school, there should be a red carpet laid out and all the kids would greet her. It was quite the opposite. She was just another student trying to get through school. She never let any of this show. There were very few times when she came home that she was down. By the time she arrived home, the manic side of her disease would come forward.

I spent time trying to discuss Alisa's issues with Paula and Tom. They would try to give me advice. Alisa was very out of control one afternoon, and I was crying after sending her to her room. I called Paula for support. She came to the house to be there for me. She asked what was going on. When I told her, she raced up the steps to Alisa's room and was yelling at her. "Why do you have to treat your mother that way?" was what I heard Paula say.

At a parent-teacher conference one year, the teacher told me that Alisa had gotten in a yelling match with another student and thrown an eraser. She missed the other student and nearly hit the teacher in the head with it. The teacher also indicated that Alisa may need mental help. The thought caught me off guard. I went home in shock to think about it.

I decided the teacher might be right when one night I was calling for Alisa and looking everywhere for her. I found her in the laundry basket in her closet. She was sobbing uncontrollably. Nothing I said seemed to comfort her. I went to get Joy, the neighbor across the street who had become close to Alisa and Debbie. Joy came, and nothing she said would calm Alisa down either. Joy suggested we take her to the emergency room. Joy drove her van while I tried to comfort my child.

By the time we got to the hospital, Alisa had calmed down quite a bit. We took her into the hospital anyway. She was checked for anything physical that could be happening. The hospital staff found nothing, so we went home. The following day, I started looking for a psychiatrist. It was difficult to find one who treated teenagers during that time. I finally found one and made an appointment.

Alisa did not want to go to the psychiatrist because she did not want people to think she was crazy. I explained to her that no one needed to know. She didn't have to tell anyone. It was our business, nobody else's. I asked her what she thought of her grandfather's diabetes. She said that it was just something Grandpa had to live with it and take his insulin. Then I asked, "What makes your illness any different from Grandpa's?" She reluctantly went to the appointment.

The psychiatrist diagnosed Alisa with depression and started her on Prozac, an antidepressant. This action caused her to become manic. She could not sleep. She acted like she was on steroids. She could not slow down. It was worse than the depression. When I called the psychiatrist to explain the reaction to the medication, he determined that she had bipolar disorder. At that time, this diagnosis was the new term for manic depression and was very rarely seen in teenagers. Most people with bipolar disorder don't experience symptoms until they are in their twenties. She was only thirteen. With a physical diagnosis, there is always hope that the patient will get better. Mental disorders are not that easy.

For me, as a parent, it was a difficult diagnosis to hear. I was devastated. How was I going to raise this child? I was determined to give her as much love and support as I could. I made sure her mind was being stimulated with new ideas all the time. When James found out about the diagnosis, he refused to believe it. He was in denial as I had been. He told me the doctors were wrong. He deflected the situation onto me and stated if I were a better parent and knew how to discipline, Alisa would be just fine. I half believed him because I was parenting based on guilt. I had taken him away from the girls, and I was trying to overcompensate for it.

It took a while for me to accept that Alisa wasn't perfect. That she was sick. Depression set in about the things she would miss. From those days until her death, I knew that she would precede me in death. My picture of her life in my mind had been going to college, getting married, finding a job that showed off her talent, and giving me grandchildren. That picture changed dramatically. I felt that Alisa would have to live in a group home or at home with me. She tried once after turning eighteen to be on her own, but that did not work out.

The next step was how to understand her disease, so I could look at the outbursts and depression as her illness. Until I did that, I took everything personally. She was attacking me when she wasn't really. I did online research, but there was little known about the disorder in teenagers. It normally manifests itself during a person's early 20s. There is so much information available nowadays. I hope that our family struggles will provide information and support for other families.

The period of diagnosis was during Alisa's years in middle school. She wanted to fit in, so she decided to take part in the school musical performances in 7th and 8th grades. She played trumpet in band and was in bell choir. She had several friends during that time.

I remember one girl who also played trumpet, and the two would practice together. They were in the musical performances together, so they practiced for that too.

Over the next four years, our life was a pattern of constant change. The doctor was trying to find a combination of drugs to treat her condition. The most prescribed drug at the time was lithium. That was one drug Alisa refused to try. We tried different psychiatrists, a total of four, all of whom confirmed the diagnosis. Over those four years, Alisa was given at least twelve different medications to try. The pattern started with a new drug by itself, but soon moved onto a combination of drugs. Alisa said some made her sleep through class while others kept her awake at night or gave her nightmares.

I finished college in the summer of 1998; however, graduation only took place in May, so I was made an official 1999 graduate. I did not want to wait until May of '99 to celebrate. I wanted the girls to know how much I appreciated their support during the long process of getting my degree. A vacation to Disney World in Florida was the answer.

We went to Florida in October after the summer rush was over. As a graduation present, my brother Harold gave us his timeshare week for that year. We stayed about a mile outside of Disney. We flew down and got checked into a suite with two bedrooms and a kitchen/living room area. It was more than we expected.

The first night I slept under the room air conditioner, and woke up with no voice. The girls were ecstatic because I wouldn't be able to keep them in line by yelling. They taunted me all day. We had a three-day pass that included Universal Studios. The first two days were in Disney. We rode a lot of the rides. Or I should say the girls rode the rides. I did go down Splash Mountain and Epcot. Debbie had to ride the Dumbo ride several times. Alisa's favorite was the teacups from *Alice in Wonderland.* We all loved Epcot. We have many pictures of the girls with the characters that roam the park. Debbie was afraid of Jafar from *Aladdin,* but let me take a picture anyway. Alisa loved them all. The best picture taken was the girls with the mice from *Cinderella.*

During that trip, we took a day and went to visit James' Aunt Joyce. She and her husband lived in St. James City. Their house sat on stilts and was surrounded by canals. Joyce and Delmar were a pair of quilters. Some of their creations won awards at quilt shows. Joyce even had one of her quilts featured on the front cover of a quilting magazine (I don't remember what the name was). They adored the girls and vice versa. Joyce was the one person in the Smith family that made me feel like I belonged. She was Richard's sister.

The girls got along fairly well during the trip. Evenings in the condo were a little tense at times because of the conflict between the girls. They were to sleep together in the second bedroom in separate beds. Alisa had trouble sleeping, causing her to be restless, and would wander around the condo, keeping Debbie awake.

We did not have lots of money to spend on food or souvenirs, so we stuck to using the grocery store. However, to make the most of the experience, I did take the girls to a Japanese steakhouse. None of us had ever been and had no idea of what the experience would be like. The surprise of the food being cooked in front of us was awesome. The chef took a liking to Alisa, and the two of them kept the rest of us laughing. At the end, the waitress gave Alisa a set of Mickey Mouse ears and dubbed her "the Japanese Minnie Mouse."

At Universal Studios, we encountered the Ghostbusters, dinosaurs from *Jurassic Park,* and the ship from *Water World.* We rode the subway through the King Kong exhibit. He was a pretty big, scary guy! Debbie screamed, and Alisa laughed. We also got to experience a tornado drawn from the *Twister* movie. We saw flying cows and vehicles being turned over. The exhibit had some wind that blew, but nothing close to a wind tornado velocity.

Debbie finished elementary school the same year Alisa completed middle school, so I hosted a mini-graduation party for them and their friends. It was held after school on the last day of school at my house. There were several teenage girls, probably 10+, running around the house. We had music and dancing in the basement, badminton in the yard, and lots of food. The girls hung out and celebrated moving forward in their school years.

I liked putting on this get-together to celebrate the closing of one chapter and the opening of another. My hope was for all the girls to have fun. I wanted them to bask in the celebration of their accomplishments. The older girls—8th-graders—had spent the school day at the pool. Alisa was burnt to a crisp. The sunburn did not stop her.

Wentzville High School was an average-sized high school. Life was changing, and so was Alisa. Her mood swings were more frequent. She had to be the center of attention much of the time. She was bullied at school sometimes. She sat at a table by herself during lunch, and the other students would make fun of her. Those feelings of hurt would not be brought home. Her journal was her release. She would be in her room just writing. I didn't read those journals until much later. It was heartbreaking to read how much pain and hurt she carried inside.

As a freshman in high school, she made the varsity cheerleading squad. This cheer team was for the hockey team. I believe that the hockey cheerleaders were considered the "throwaways" from the football and basketball cheerleaders and, therefore, not really thought of as cheerleaders. I didn't go to many games, but I did, at least once, to see her. This squad took third place in the state competition. During that competition, she experienced her first menstrual cycle. She told me after using the bathroom, but it didn't even phase her. She had figured out what to do on her own or with help from another cheerleader. I was more anxious about the situation than she was. I never had to have "the talk" with her.

Alisa did well in school. She placed second in the school science fair during her freshman year. She was very smart, so I did not see her studying very often. Her mind would just absorb the material presented. She did love to read, which helped with her schoolwork. Her grades were good, and she usually made the honor roll. She did procrastinate on writing papers. She would leave the paper until the night before it was due, then stay up all night to complete it. This method always seemed to work for her. She received recognition for language arts, science, and social studies in 2000. She was part of the swim team and ran track.

I always tried to treat the girls the same, but with Alisa's condition, she was a high-maintenance child. When she was not with me, I was terrified of what she could be doing. I wanted my girls to have every opportunity to try whatever interested them. Debbie's interests were art classes, gymnastics, band, and choir. Alisa was cheerleading, acting, gymnastics, swim team, track, and choir. She did play trumpet in middle school, but dropped out of band after two years.

To have a little fun during my vacations, I would plan a getaway. Most years, we did not go anywhere, but one summer we went to the Lake of the Ozarks for a four-day weekend. The trip was a pretty good one. It rained, but that was okay. It meant that the three of us could try to bond a little. We played games and just hung out. Alisa was taking her medications. We all relaxed and enjoyed our time together.

During our time in Wentzville, we would spend time with Paula, Tom, and their kids. Elizabeth was older, and Alisa looked up to her. They were not close, but they were cousins just the same. Joe was four months younger than Alisa, which made them good playmates. We would go to Paula's on the weekend sometimes. Paula was less tolerant of Alisa's behavior, so a portion of these visits would be less than pleasant. I began to withdraw from Paula and Tom due to Alisa's behavior. I felt I was being judged by the way she acted. Both families were getting busier with the kids' schedules, school, and work.

We always had Thanksgiving and Christmas with Paula and Tom. Because food and presents were involved, these holidays went pretty well. When Tom carved the turkey, all the kids would fight over the skin. There was a lot of laughter and many unusual dinner conversations.

For her eleventh birthday, Alisa wanted a dog. We went to an adoption event and found Holly and Duke, her brother. She wanted to adopt both, but that was not an option. Getting one dog with two nearly teenage girls in the house was about all I thought I could handle. Holly was a six-month-old German Shepherd mix. We had to put her in the car to get her home. She resisted. It took all three of us to finally push her in. When we got home, Holly ran upstairs and hid in the bathroom. We realized that Holly must have been abused. She was a good guard dog. She did not like men or newspapers. We made this assumption about her when Debbie started delivering papers on Fridays. When we brought the papers in, Holly would run and hide.

Alisa was good with animals. Strays were attracted to her. We had many strays she brought home during her life. We had many cats and dogs. In Wentzville, the strays were mainly cats. It wasn't until later that the dogs started coming. As she grew older, she stopped bringing home stray animals. She began to bring home stray people. She wanted to help as many people as she could. She often gave away her clothes.

There is a student ambassador program called People to People. Its purpose is to take American teenagers to visit other counties to help build an understanding of other cultures. Alisa was selected to participate in that program and represent the U.S. in Spain, Italy, and France. I drove her to the meetings, where she had to learn about the different cultures and their norms so she would not say or do something wrong for that culture.

To raise the funds needed to go, Alisa started taking odd jobs. She had a babysitting job every day after school. She also started working as an assistant at Stacey's Gymnastics, where she used to take lessons. Alisa asked James to contribute. He felt sending a thirteen-year-old to Europe was a bad idea, but he did help the cause. Alisa did get some donations as well. I contributed what I could, and we finally made the goal amount so she could go.

On June 19th, 1999, I drove Alisa to the airport and waited inside with her to make sure nothing happened. After I was sure that she had connected with the group and had her plane ticket, I went back to my car and cried. What had I done? Sending my daughter off to a foreign land at such a young age? By now, I knew that she was going to have problems. I was on edge the whole time she was gone. She was allowed to call a few times. She got sick in Spain, and the chaperone called me to see if there was anything she was allergic to. The chaperone was going to give her a pill (which I approved), but Alisa had never been able to swallow a pill. Somehow, the chaperone got the pill down her. She lost her retainer for her braces in Spain. She bought me a necklace of emeralds shaped like a butterfly. When she returned, she wrote an article for the local newspaper about her adventures.

The following was written on notecards as if she had to give a speech:

"First, I would like to thank you for your donation. I had an experience that most kids only dream about. I had a great time. I learned a lot, too.

My trip started on June 19th. The flight to Madrid was the longest and most boring I had ever been on.

That night in Madrid, we took a short tour before retiring back to our hotels. The next day I had a piea. A piea is a Spanish meal made of all kinds of seafood such as crab, mussels, octopus tentacles, and much more. They gave me a live crab that walked off my plate.

The next course was Tortia. It was good. It is just a burrito wrapper thing. That same day, I learned about Don Quixote and Concho.

On June 21st, we started early to get to Toledo, the town of swords. There we toured many cathedrals, including the Toledo Cathedral. Toledo Cathedral was once bigger than St. Peter's Cathedral, but the Pope said nothing could be larger than St. Peter's Cathedral. Toledo Cathedral had to be made smaller.

Also, in Spain, I got a special treat called a Tapa. A tapa is a Spanish dessert, kind of like a cream puff. It's a very small sandwich with chocolate cream in the middle and chocolate swirled on top.

That night, I was very happy because I got to participate in the traditional Flamenco dance. It is a style of dancing created by the Spanish.

On June 27th, we left for Barcelona, where we had lunch at the Hard Rock Café and then swam in the 1992 Olympic pool.

It was on to France, and our first day there, we learned about a saltwater plant that, if you eat it, it really tastes like salt. We learned this and a spikey porcupine plant named 'Junkus' at a nature center.

Then on June 30th, we went to home stays for three days. I learned while there, three main things: Never play chess with a French girl. They will always win.

Guys at the pool are not allowed to wear swim trunks. They only wear Speedos. Guys are not afraid of showing what they've got, but don't ask how I know that.

The last important thing I found out in France were:

Nutella—a chocolate spread for a baguette.

I learned about the nose at Fragonard's perfumery. The nose tests all the perfumes and then studies their makeup for years. He is not allowed to drink or smoke ever.

Onward hoe! Italy, here we come. The first day in Italy, we went to the Leaning Tower of Pisa. I tried to hold it up, but my arms got tired. We saw lots of origins of people. We saw Chinese, Gypsies and even people from Holland.

While in Italy, I had the famous gelati. A tremendously tasty type of ice cream you can only find in Italy.

The night after Pisa, I took an Italian cooking class. I liked it overall, but the bread spreads were gross.

Also, while in Italy, I saw a lot of Michelangelo's work, especially *David*. I learned about the Medici family and how Michelangelo came about. I saw the Colosseum, where the Romans had battles for pleasure. I saw the catacombs where early Christians are buried. I actually went four stories underground to see their graves.

The last place we went before our journey home was Vatican City. I went to St. Peter's Church, where I met the Pope (John Paul II), and he blessed my Rosary. I saw the Trevi Fountain and the Pantheon. At the Trevi Fountain, we threw two coins in the fountain—one for a wish and the other to come back someday. The Pantheon is just a historical Roman building where the Romans would have a council.

I was very excited to go home and tell my mom everything I had learned. But my smiles turned quickly to tears as I thought of all the things I would miss. I made many friends and had many adventures. I will remember this trip forever.

Europe was one of the greatest things to happen to me. I owe it all to my mother who, along with me, worked her butt off to help me get there."

When Alisa was thirteen, after she came back from Europe, she took acting classes at John Robert Powers, which is a talent and modeling agency. This meant driving her to meetings and rehearsals at least once a week. The trip would take about half an hour each way. I would either stay there or go to the nearest mall and walk around. She loved acting. She had big dreams of fame, fortune, adventure, and being loved.

She spent many hours in her room or out in the yard rehearsing her parts. When she thought she was ready, she would perform in front of me. She was very good. I think these acting classes may have helped her hide her disease. There were many times when I could not tell if she was telling me the truth or just putting on an act.

She was selected to go to the International Modeling and Talent Association's yearly talent contest in Los Angeles in January of 2000. (The contest is better known as IMTA.) John Robert Powers flew us to LA and paid for our stay in the Hotel Westin Bonaventure. The hotel is located near the famous Wilshire Boulevard and Rodeo Drive shopping district. It had a rooftop restaurant that rotated 360 degrees so you could see the whole city. Alisa was quite excited about being that close to all the Hollywood action. One night, the contestants had dinner in the restaurant, which Alisa enjoyed.

The contest ran for five days, which gave us time for a little fun. We went to Universal Studios, where actual movies are made. Not to be confused with the amusement parks of the same name in Florida. We saw how the towns of the old Western movies were made small to make the actors look larger than life during filming. The sets were just stand-up boards painted on one side to look like storefronts and were propped up in the back. We even saw a miniature version of the set for the movie *Waterworld*.

There were over two hundred girls in Alisa's age group. In the competition, she placed 6th in her division. She had high expectations for herself, so coming in at 6th place was quite the blow. The contest only took the first five in each division. She felt she had failed. I told her that coming in 6th was great. To be that high up, when there were more than two hundred others competing, should give her a sense of pride. She could not see it that way. She was given a black ribbon for "Competition Excellence," which she felt was a poor consolation prize.

She wanted to continue acting. She auditioned for and was accepted as part of the cast of Henry Fielding's *Tom Jones* at the Florissant Civic Center Theater. She was cast as Nancy, one of the town women. Again, I would drive her to rehearsals and wait for her to come out. I did get involved with the production and worked behind the scenes to help pass the time. I helped with stage setup and costumes.

The play ran from April 7th through the 16th, but it was not every night. Her grandparents came out to see her perform on the 15th, along with Uncle Tom and Aunt Paula. She was excited to have family come to her show. James did not come. At the end of the performance that night, we all gave her flowers. In her scrapbook, there is a note that on the last night of the show there was tornado in the area. The cast had to go through a passage to get under the stage and into the orchestra pit for safety.

Renaissance fairs were popular with both girls. We experienced our first fair while James and I were still married. In Colorado, the fair runs every weekend through the month of June. James was interested in this type of cultural experience, so he was more engaged than usual. James had dressed for the event by wearing knee-high lace-up moccasins and a billowy off-white shirt. We walked around visiting all the vendor booths. We listened to strolling minstrels and ate turkey legs. The high point of the day occurred in the afternoon. All would be summoned to the joisting area. The king and his court were seated next to the rink (corral). When summoned by the king, the knights, dressed in chain mail, would come riding at each other on horseback and try to knock the opponent off their horse.

Wentzville did not have a Renaissance fair the first year we lived there. A year or two later, the fair got underway outside of town. The first year the girls and I attended, we were just visitors. Alisa struck up a conversation with members of the court. The following year, both Alisa and Debbie were invited to be part of the cast. Alisa was an apple thief, and Debbie was a fairy. Another year, Alisa was part of the court. I had made their costumes. I made myself one as well because I had to be on-site whenever the girls were there. I remember making costumes for other fairies. I enjoyed making them. I entertained the idea of making some and selling them at the fair.

The Renaissance fair in Wentzville took place in early summer. The weather could be quite unpredictable, but most of the time it was hot and humid. The costumes were made from heavy upholstery fabric, making the days seem long sometimes. The experience of being transported back in time became something we all looked forward to. The adventure was a pleasant way to spend a summer day.

The summer of 2000 meant concerts with friends and day camps while I worked. Alisa went to cheerleading camp at the end of June through the beginning of July. The first night at camp, Alisa did not feel well. She called me and asked me to come and get her. I told her to tough it out and give it a chance. She did.

By the end of camp, she was glad she had stayed. The last day of camp, the girls gave a performance for the parents. Alisa had made a lot of progress since her days of cheering for the little league football team. My heart felt like it would explode with pride. She was given an award at camp for outstanding effort and performance.

The camp also had included a day at Triangle Y Ranch, where the girls got to ride horses and help on the ranch. She enjoyed riding the horses and participating on the ranch. From her scrapbook: "Alex from

Germany taught us horse parts and saddle parts. Greg from the U.S. taught us to walk and trot in circles and reverses."

Debbie went to day camps due to her age. Her camps were focused on soccer. She enjoyed playing; however, she was not an aggressive player at first. She was in soccer for several seasons. She gained confidence, and she was soon able to charge ahead toward the goal. She stopped being afraid of the other players coming at her.

The concerts we attended included Charlie Daniels Band, Backstreet Boys, and John Mellencamp. I know these concerts weren't all in 2000, but I lumped them together. The concerts were always a good time. The Mellencamp concert was special for a couple of reasons. It was the grand opening of a small concert venue in St. Charles: The Family Arena. It was Alisa's 13th birthday. We all had fun, danced, and sang. It was a very pleasant evening.

The girls went to James' in Denver for their summer visit after Alisa returned from Europe. During the visit, Alisa kept a "summer record" of their activities. James took them to Elitch Gardens on Monday (now Six Flags) and to see *Mission: Impossible II* on Tuesday. He went back to work on Wednesday, and Alisa spent the day cleaning and swimming at the apartment complex's pool. The rest of the "record" she talks about spending a lot of time with James' new girlfriend and her children, DJ, Logan, and Dustin. She says they "slept over" at DJ's. On Saturday, they all went to the Renaissance fair in Larkspur.

The girls were to come home Sunday, but somehow, they missed their flight. It was scheduled to leave at 5:35 P.M. They were rebooked and made it home the next night. How do you miss a late afternoon flight? I was angry. I played the scenario in reverse. If they had missed their outgoing flight, James would have done something, even if it was only shouting.

Debbie and Alisa had a love-hate relationship. Deep down, they knew they loved each other and were there for each other. I have videos of the two of them playing sumo wrestling. They had strapped throw pillows to their bellies and were bouncing off from each other. The sound of their laughter in that video still makes me laugh, remembering how special their relationship was.

We had a small hill (slope, really) behind the house, and during the winter, the sled would come out, and down they went. Sometimes, each would take their turn alone, but many times they rode down together. We had a telephone junction box at the corner of the property. One afternoon, they decided they wanted to try to hit it. Third time down the hill, Alisa did, head first. Debbie had fallen off the back, the sled made a 180-degree turn and slammed into the box. The laughter was contagious. I have that on video as well.

The boys in the neighborhood would hang around the house. They would play with Alisa, but sometimes make fun of Debbie. When they saw my car coming down the street, they would scatter. I remember an incident involving the two boys who lived across the creek. I cannot remember exactly what it was, but Alisa had gotten the boys in trouble, so they were grounded from our house for a short while.

We, as a family, tried to live a normal life, but it was difficult. I am trying to keep this writing from being too negative. Debbie got a weekly paper route. Friday nights, we would pick up the papers and then roll them, put them in clear bags, and deliver. The route was around Lake St. Louis, so I drove, and she flung. Sometimes Joe would go with us. He and Debbie would have contests to see who could throw farther or who could hit the mailbox.

Alisa got invited to sleepovers. She was friends with most of the cheerleaders on her squad. Her school friends were Christy and Danielle. She had one close cheerleader as a friend. Her name was Laurie. She was older and could drive.

I did not allow the girls to date until they got older. That generation doesn't date anyway except for big events like homecoming and prom. The kids just hang out together. I made an exception for one homecoming dance. Wes asked Alisa to go in 2000. Wes was a boy from another neighborhood. The girls passed his house on the way home from school each day. I guess all went well. Alisa took pictures of her friends, and someone took a picture of her and Wes. She was fourteen.

With all that the girls were involved in, I decided it was time for Alisa to get a cellphone. She was very excited about having it. After Alisa told her dad, James called and chewed me out. "She is only fourteen, why does she need a cellphone? Is that just a random age that you decided on?" I tried to explain that all the activities she was in, I needed to be able to get in touch with her. James didn't agree. I felt James was trying to control me again.

We lived in Wentzville for four years. I gained confidence during that time about my ability to be a good parent. There were many times when Alisa was having an episode that I would question if I were capable enough to handle this child. Little did I know the worst was yet to come.

# CHAPTER NINE
## *NY Adventure*

The world turned upside down in early 2001. My dad, Bill, was diagnosed with lung cancer and was given three to six months to live. He refused treatment. The doctor told him that the treatment would just prolong the agony and would not really help because he was terminal. Dad stated that if he was going to feel like he had been feeling in recent years, then he was satisfied not to undergo treatment.

I had been trying to sell the house in Wentzville to buy something bigger, but there was no interest. I see now that God played His hand in that process. I was supposed to go to New York to be with Dad. We packed up the house to move to NY. Adam came to load and drive the truck. I left the for-sale sign up with instructions to the realtor to keep the listing active. The house finally sold in May.

I was sad to leave the house we had built together, but in the long run, I was not sad to leave Missouri. It was too hot. I was driving on I-70 in rush-hour traffic at a complete standstill in front of the mall. The mall sign said it was 112 degrees. I had the air conditioning cranked all the way up and was still sweating.

I felt it was important to move to New York so that the girls could spend more time with Grandpa and Grandma Colten. I had only taken the girls to NY a few times. They knew all about Grandma and Grandpa Smith, but almost nothing about my parents. It was a good time for them to bond.

I enrolled the girls in school to finish the school year. Some of the teachers I had were still teaching, so Debbie had one of the teachers I had: Mrs. Goff. Debbie enjoyed the subject and Mrs. Goff. I don't think Alisa had the same experience.

The move to NY was a culture shock for both girls. Debbie just rolled with it, but the changes made a huge impression on Alisa. She was used to hallways jammed with students and large class sizes. Sidney High School is not that big. She made friends and did well in school.

Alisa had taken up playing trumpet in MO, but when we moved to NY, she stopped playing. She quit because of the teacher. I am not sure why. All Alisa said was that she did not like playing anymore due to a change in expectations from the teacher. I was sorry that this happened. She really liked playing. It may have kept her focused.

I had gotten us a three-bedroom apartment on the main floor of the building. The apartment complex was older, so sounds carried. Alisa and I started getting into a lot more arguments. I would try to keep my voice down, but Alisa would escalate quickly, leading to much yelling. I would send her to her room to cool off.

Her new friends encouraged Alisa to start sneaking out at night. She started smoking cigarettes, which led to smoking weed. Friends would show up at her window, and off she would go. She wanted to party by drinking and hanging out. There is not much to do in Upstate NY. The kids would hang out in a field and build bonfires and smoke pot. They would go swimming in the local water hole. There are many old train trestles in the area, which are left standing from the early 1900s, when the area was thriving. The kids would jump from the trestle into the swimming hole. I have never been there but have been told it is a high trestle. Good way to break an arm or leg or your skull.

Alisa had a couple of friends. One girl, I can't remember what her name was, and then there was Jamie. The first girl was the wild child and would get Alisa to go to the field or her house. Jamie seemed more responsible. She had Alisa spend the night with her. Pictures showed a normal teenage sleepover. However, with the first girl, I believe that the Sidney Police force got to know Alisa.

Sidney is a town of about 4,000 people and covers approximately two and a half square miles. Many nights, Alisa would be out "walking" the streets of Sidney. I was concerned about her being out late. I wasn't in a panic as I would have been in Wentzville. The worst that could happen was she could get picked up by the cops and brought back home.

One afternoon after school, Alisa came home and we started arguing. She had gotten angry over something I said. Maybe I told her she couldn't hang out with her friends. I don't remember. I do remember her screaming. She went into the kitchen, grabbed a knife, and threatened to stab me. Debbie called 911, but before the police could arrive, she left through her bedroom window. I was in a panic. I lay in bed awake, waiting for news. She had been picked up by the police.

She was taken to Fox Hospital, where she spent a few days on the psychiatric floor. People with mental disorders are often put in a psychiatric ward on a 72-hour hold. This usually means the behavior displayed indicates the person was a threat to someone or to themselves. The patient has to stay and be evaluated for mental illness. No one can have them released until the doctor clears them at the end of the hold. This was the first of many times that hospitalization or incarceration would occur.

I found out later that Alisa was having trouble "watching Grandpa die," as she put it. She did not have the coping skills to handle the situation. It got worse when I got a job. I worked in Binghamton, which is about an hour's drive. I worked as a programmer converting assembler code to COBOL. I bring this up because it affected my feeling of confidence in my ability to do the job. I had never really understood assembler code, so converting it to COBOL was difficult. This overflowed into my confidence in being able to raise my girls. I was coping with my own feelings about losing my father. Alisa must have sensed both my coping with Dad and the insecurity about the job. She continued to defy me.

A major plus side to this adventure was that I got to reconnect with my best friend for life. We had met in middle school and have been friends ever since. We had drifted apart not only due to distance, but we were starting families. We were able to pick up right where we left off. Her name is Kathy.

The girls got to know more about their uncles. Alisa got close to her Aunt Ann and Uncle Jordan. Uncle Henry became a favorite. There was a swimming hole in the creek behind his house. The girls would go over to swim or just float and relax. Henry told me that he learned what a great set of girls I had during that time. He described Alisa lying on a flotation device, smoking a joint, and just chilling out.

My father was an incredibly unique individual with old-fashioned ways. He was quite the joker. One example was about Alisa getting her hair done. She had a friend who was in cosmetology class and wanted to do Alisa's hair. Alisa came back to Grandma's house with orange hair. Dad looked at her and asked if the hairdo came with an umbrella, "cause it sure is a pisser."

I felt positive about the relationship that the girls got to have with him before he passed. It was a hard six-month period, but I don't regret taking the detour in our lives. Each girl had time to bond with Grandpa before he passed away. I do feel guilty about leaving to go back to Colorado in August. I felt I was running away. I couldn't handle watching Dad die either. He was getting worse, so I used the excuse that the girls needed to get settled to go back to school in Colorado.

My Dad died in October of 2001, so it was back to NY for the funeral. We could not afford to fly, so road trip it was. The drive is normally about 28-30 hours to complete the trip. All three of us drove and got home within that timeframe. After having time to get to know Grandpa Colten, Alisa and Debbie were both very upset. They were, however, there for me. They literally held me up during the graveside service. Not being close to my father, I was surprised by the level of grief I felt.

# CHAPTER TEN

## *2001-2006*

The following narrative is coming from my memory and physical documents, like the Aurora Police blotter. I want to make clear that from January of 2002 until October of 2014, life for me was one big blur. Every day was a new challenge. I lived from crisis to crisis. I have to write about the good times we had on vacations, just to have a positive perspective on our lives.

I believe what I outline next is true, but the timing of things may be out of order. Some events my mind won't allow me to remember specific details. This part will cover 2001-2006 to the best of my ability. I use certain situations as milestones to try to keep things straight in my head.

We moved back to Colorado in August 2001. We did not have a place to live, and I had no job. James took Alisa to his house. My friend Joan took Debbie and me in. Many things happened quickly, including police involvement. I have a police blotter, which is a summary listing of the contact with police that a person has. I obtained a copy of the blotter from the Aurora Police Department, which outlines all the encounters between Alisa and them. In total, there are 48 entries. Several are the same offense, like ten speeding tickets. I am not going to list every single one, but I will refer to them in the following pages.

James had a new wife: Tina. Tina had a young daughter (Shelly) and a toddler (Mark). Shelly lived with James and Tina, so the household became four. Mark lived in Utah with his grandparents (maybe, not really sure). Alisa became a big sister to Shelly. Shelly was used to getting her own way. Being a big sister to Shelly was exciting for Alisa until she started feeling neglected because Shelly got all the attention.

Also in the household was at least one dog. Within a month of her arrival, the dog chewed the nose off from Mr. Fuzzykins (remember him?). Alisa was heartbroken. When she came for a visit, she brought him and asked if I could fix him. I am pretty good with a needle and thread, so I tried. When I finished, he was far from perfect, but he no longer had a hole in his face. I mention Mr. Fuzzykins specifically to point out that someone with bipolar will attach themselves to items that make them feel loved and grounded. Alisa still had Mr. Fuzzykins and that simple square quilt I had made in Florida in her car when I went to retrieve it. She always knew that these were signs of my love for her.

James enrolled her in Legacy High School, which is in a high-class neighborhood. The kids wore designer clothes and drove expensive cars to school. Alisa tried to blend in and make friends. She joined choir. She liked to sing, so she thought this would help her fit in. She was very good and got a solo in the Christmas show. However, neither James nor Tina would pick her up after choir practice. "If she wants after-school activities, she can find her own way home. We're not going to change our lives around for her." The school was across the busy highway of I-25, about three or four miles from the house.

Alisa started asking other kids for rides home. She met a lot of people that way, and some had bad reputations. She got into the wrong crowd. Her best friends were Jackie and Victoria. She had other people she hung out with, but these were the ones she spent the most time with. Jackie lived in a trailer park while Victoria lived in a house near the high school.

I mention the girls by name because I remember incidents that happened when Alisa was spending time with each of them. During one of the visits to Jackie's, a bunch of the girls got together and started taunting a girl named Cassandra. She was overweight and had a loud mouth. Of course, the gang of girls made fun of her weight and other things. A fight ensued between Alisa and Cassandra, with a lot of kicking and punching. When police arrived, Alisa had Cassandra on the ground and had given her a black eye.

Alisa was given a ticket for assault by the Broomfield Police. In court, she received a deferred sentence and community service. There was also a restraining order in place from Cassandra. A deferred sentence meant if she stayed out of trouble for a year, the charges would be dropped. Besides the incident in NY, when she was taken to the hospital, I believe this was Alisa's first contact with police.

Alisa had many more encounters with the Aurora Police than I knew of. She also had a lot of contact with the Arapahoe County Sheriff's Office. Many times, there would be a case in Aurora that would be combined with a county case, so the county would take over. There are some years on the police blotter that do not have entries. During those times, she was in jail, in rehab, on probation, or was under Arapahoe County jurisdiction. When she was on probation, she always managed to fly under the police radar, staying out of trouble.

Finding a place for community service was difficult. The court had given her a list of places to go to. Places that normally let kids do community service don't allow anyone with assault charges to work at their place. After meeting with the court representative about this issue, Alisa was assigned to make dresses for the girls in domestic violence shelters.

Sewing was not something Alisa had shown any interest in, so I got to teach her the basics. She was impatient with herself and would get easily frustrated. Pinning and cutting the pattern would be fine, but sewing the dress together got her upset. She didn't like the machine. Sewing a straight line was difficult for her. I remember learning to sew, so I understood her position. I patiently kept working with her. Each dress had a zipper. Zippers can be tricky, especially for a beginner. After much arguing and refusal to work on the dresses, we came to an agreement. She would make the dress, and I would put in the zippers. Worked for us. She had to complete 20-25 (?) within a three-month period. It was hard, but we made the deadline. I'm not sure that making dresses had any effect on modifying her behavior.

September 11, 2001, started with a phone call from James. September $11^{th}$ is his birthday. He told me to turn on the news. Joan had gone to D.C. for work, and I was helping Dean with their son Toby. I know how that day affected me. I was paralyzed with disbelief. When Debbie got home from school, she said they had the TV on all day in the classroom. She was as devastated as was the rest of the country. Since Alisa was living at James', I never knew how this tragedy had affected her. I don't ever remember talking to her about it. For me, having been raised in NY, I felt like part of my heart had been torn out. The first plane had just hit the north tower when I turned on the news. I was just in time to see the second plane hit the south tower. That image is implanted in my brain forever.

Alisa turned fifteen while living with James and Tina. Tina was into smoking pot. Being a new stepmom (she and James had gotten married in the spring that year), Tina wanted to get Alisa's approval, so Tina started sharing her pot with Alisa. She would let Alisa drive her car even though she wasn't old enough to get a permit. Lots of good lessons learned when living up there.

One day, shortly before Thanksgiving, James came home early from work to walk into a pot-smelling house. He was angry and asked what was going on. Tina blamed Alisa for smoking even though Tina was doing so as well. James kicked Alisa out. It had been about three months. He called me and said I had to take her because he had his family, meaning Tina and Shelly, to protect. Come and get her.

As I drove to pick Alisa up, I felt a sense of dread with the idea of trying to be a good full-time parent to her again. I did not have to be worrying daily about what she was doing while at James'. I felt other things as well. I had been angered by the comment James made about having to protect his family. What did he consider Alisa? She was more family than Tina and Shelly. Debbie told me recently that she felt James had replaced her and Alisa with Shelly and Tina during that time.

I had gotten a two-bedroom apartment by this time. This meant Alisa and Debbie had to share a bedroom for the first time in their lives. They had always had separate rooms, except when Debbie was first born. This was quite an adjustment. Debbie would try to sleep, and Alisa would be up late. She didn't need much sleep due to her bipolar disorder. She could go days with less than five hours of sleep a night. There was a lot of fighting over this. Debbie usually ended up in bed with me.

Alisa wanted to finish the semester at Legacy. I agreed that she shouldn't change school mid-semester. Every morning and every afternoon, I would drive through rush-hour traffic about thirty miles to take her to school and pick her up. Sometimes she would stay with Jackie or Victoria. She started walking out of school prior to 2nd period. By the time I got back home, the school would be calling to say that Alisa had missed one or more of her classes that day. She would leave with friends and go to smoke pot at somebody's house. Victoria's house was a common hangout.

Alisa asked if we could meet in a strip mall parking lot on 104th Avenue when I picked her up. She did not want me to know who she was with or where she had been. We had missed connections at times due to it being November and December. She would say "I'm at the Home Depot," but would be near Old Navy. Same strip mall, just different ends. It wouldn't have been such a big deal if it was summer, and we could see each other.

One afternoon, however, I picked her up closer to Legacy High School. She was hungry, so we went through a Wendy's drive-thru. As we were making our way to Wendy's, we started to fight. We got the food and started to leave. I was waiting to turn out of the parking lot, when Alisa jumped out of the car and started running. During the next hour or so, I chased her all over Westminster. She was running through people's backyards and jumping fences to stay off the street, so I couldn't find her. It was cold. There was snow on the ground. She only had on a hoodie.

Alisa finally came to her senses and told me to pick her up at some intersection. I got there. She got in the car. She was still angry, so she yelled at me most of the way home. Even though I hadn't personally seen her jumping fences, I have an image in my mind of her leaping a fence that will never leave me. I have blocked out a lot of that night due to the terror in my heart, but when I think about it, I get a strong feeling of terror and anguish.

Christmas and New Year's came and went without incident. The girls spent time with James during the holidays. Debbie and Alisa began to fight more often about sharing a room. Police contact would soon be commonplace.

January 13, 2002, was the first Aurora Police encounter. The girls had been fighting. I tried to de-escalate the situation but was unable to. Alisa left through the sliding glass door on the patio while I was blocking the apartment's main entrance. I called the police and reported her as a runaway. She was brought home.

The next encounter on the police blotter shows an incident of disturbing the peace/disorderly conduct. It occurred a month after the runaway, February 11, 2002. I never knew about this. I don't think she was arrested. Police may have just given her a warning or ticket.

James would not come to Aurora to pick up the girls for his weekend visitation. I was always responsible to make the trek to the northwest side of town to deliver them. On one of the return trips, the transmission went out in my van. We were still on the northwest side of town. I called James. He came to help by calling a tow truck and getting the van to a shop for service. Now I was without a vehicle. Tina was not working at the time. She suggested that I take her car and use it while mine was in the shop. She wanted to keep things civil as she adjusted to being a stepmom. I was very leery about taking it, but I had no other choice since I could not afford a rental car. Little did I know that she had been giving

Alisa driving lessons in that car, even though Alisa was fifteen and not old enough to drive. I took the car back to the apartment.

One symptom of bipolar disorder is the ability to go long periods without sleep, then sleep 24 hours straight. Alisa would do many things during the late-night/early morning hours while I was asleep. On February 25th, 2002, while I had Tina's car, Alisa got lonely and stole it. I always keep my keys on a key rack near the door. She got up, grabbed the keys, and left. She felt she could drive the car since Tina had let her drive it before.

Around midnight, I got a call from James saying Alisa had been in an accident. I thought he was joking. I had to go into the girls' room and do a bed check to confirm what he was saying. When I returned to the phone, James said she was okay, just shaken up a bit.

She had picked up her friend Victoria. They smoked some pot. They went cruising around Broomfield/Westminster. It was snowing that night. Alisa came to the stoplight at 120th and Washington. The light turned red, but she couldn't stop. She hit a light pole. Both girls were wearing seatbelts. Victoria had asthma, and when she was restrained by the seatbelt, the impact triggered an asthma attack. She was taken by ambulance to a hospital, where she stayed overnight. After that night, Alisa never wore a seatbelt again. I started sleeping with the keys under my pillow.

I could not go to the scene since I had no vehicle. I had to trust James and Tina to make the right decisions. Alisa was allowed to go to James' for the night. I believe he took her to court the next day. She was charged with aggravated motor vehicle theft valued at over $15,000. As part of her sentence, she had to pay restitution to Tina for the $500 deductible on the insurance.

From August 2001 until March of 2002, I worked three jobs just to pay the bills and keep a roof over our heads. I remember doing so because I applied for Medicaid and was denied. I made too much money. Then, in March, with the help of my friend Joan, I was offered a position with Kaiser Permanente as a programmer using a language I did not know. The boss knew I did not know the language when she hired me. She felt it would take less time for me to learn the language and start building reports than it would be to go through formal channels to get the reports from IT she wanted. I spent much of that work time just learning the language. I thought I was pretty good for being self-taught.

In 2003, Kaiser made the decision to install Epic software. For those who do not know what Epic is, it is a very complex software system used by hospitals and doctor offices for everything from scheduling to billing. It was one of the first big electronic medical records systems. In 2003, Epic was a small company with few clients until they signed a contract with Kaiser.

No one within Kaiser knew anything about the software. All the people chosen for the Epic team were going to Madison, Wisconsin, to be certified. I was chosen to be the professional billing guru. I was sent to Wisconsin many times between February and July of 2003. At the end of each course, you had to take a certification test. Depending on the course, you also had to complete a sample project using the software you had just learned. Having this knowledge would be quite an asset in the years ahead.

I think I started working at Kaiser the first part of March 2002. After starting work for Kaiser, Alisa's behavior really started to change. I don't know if she was taking medication at that time. I know when she lived with James for those three months, he had not made her take any. He said she didn't need it. She was starting to get into trouble a lot. There is a police blotter entry for March 31st indicating larceny for shoplifting. I was not aware of this.

I haven't included much about Debbie in this writing up to now because she was my rock. She was always there to support me. She didn't back-talk or get into trouble. I don't remember her ever getting into trouble until high school. The time is right now to add her to this rambling. I know I put her through so much, and sometimes I wish I could go back and change things with her.

Life became more dramatic. I had to be at work by 7:30, which was before the girls had to be at school. The neighbor upstairs in the apartment building, whose daughter went to the same school as Debbie (Columbia Middle School), would take Debbie to school. Alisa had been enrolled in Rangeview during winter break and started in January. I took her to school those first couple of months. By the time I started work at Kaiser, Alisa had made some friends who would give her rides to school. An added note here, I changed the ringtone on my phone to be a siren whenever Alisa would call.

Alisa started dating Ben from Legacy High School. (I have to make clear who this Ben was because she got another Ben later on.) I remember Ben coming down to the apartment to take her out. When they got back to the apartment, they were sitting in the car for quite a while. I went out to tell her she had to come in, to find she was using her hand to perform a sexual act on Ben. She was not at all embarrassed. I was. We discussed her action later and proceeded to tell me about James' vast collection of pornographic materials. I was shocked. I had lived with the man for more than ten years and had never seen any sign of porn. Maybe that was what he was watching on the computer all those nights he would stay up. Then maybe he would find some girl to pursue conversation with about what he was seeing, or go to a chat room for a little stimulation. Alisa said that James and Tina were very open about their sex life. "Oh, yeah, they go in the bedroom and lock the door. I can always hear them."

The apartment complex had a pool. One warm night (April 13, 2002), Alisa asked to go to the pool. I said yes, but told her to be home by 10 P.M. Ten o'clock came, and no Alisa. I waited until 10:15, then I went to look for her. When I got her out of the pool, she was enraged, telling me I had embarrassed her in front of her friends. That was a night from hell. She threw things, swore at me, and Debbie. I tried to take her cellphone away from her, but we ended up in a physical brawl on the floor. I yelled for Debbie to call the police. Before the police arrived, Alisa bit me on the left wrist hard enough that her teeth marks showed on my arm for about a week.

The Aurora Police came and tried to talk her down. They stated that if she did not calm down that she could be arrested for assault. She finally calmed down enough so the police would leave. The calm did not last. She was good at saying the right thing at the right time. The police were called again, and she was arrested for assault and battery. She was transported to the juvenile detention center known as the Foote Center.

She would call almost every day to ask if I would bail her out. I never did. I would visit when allowed and bring her Snickers ice cream bars, which comforted her while she was going through withdrawal. I watched her detox in jail. She had been using cocaine. Now, without it, she was in physical and emotional pain. She wanted me to bail her out so she could find another fix. Since it was a juvenile facility, I was allowed to be in the room with her. (Adult jails use video monitors for visits using a phone to talk.) I would sit and talk to her and hug her. I always reminded her that I loved her. She again would ask if I would bail her out. The answer was always no.

After Alisa's stay at the Foote Center, she was sent to a facility on the west side of town. I don't remember the name, but I know it was on the grounds of Fort Logan. The facility was actually a large house with several girls staying there. I think it was supposed to be a halfway house, maybe. It seemed more like a sorority house than a place of discipline.

I could visit on certain days and before a certain curfew time, which I remember as being early. I would leave after work to drive across town in rush-hour traffic to see Alisa. I hated the drive. There was no easy way to get there, so I sat at many red lights during the rush hour. There were a couple of times that I got held up in traffic, meaning I was later than curfew, so I wasn't allowed to see her. I got angry often during those drives. I blamed her for not taking her medication, which is why she ended up there. I was always on edge.

Between the Foote Center and Fort Logan, I don't remember how long she was out of the house, but I know it wasn't long. The staff at Fort Logan did some counseling, but the biggest benefit of her being there, she was made to take her medication. This was the first of many detention/rehabilitation facilities we would deal with.

Being released from Fort Logan, Alisa got a job working for the city as a lifeguard. She was fifteen. She met her best friend, Audrey, while working at the pools. The two became very close. I was very happy that Alisa and Audrey were friends. I felt Audrey could have a positive influence on her. Audrey was not into drugs that I knew of, but she did drink.

Audrey was as beautiful as Alisa, so they were constantly being approached for their looks. They worked a lot of shifts together at the Delmar and Utah pools. One Sunday afternoon, both were working when a rather large man started flailing for help. Both jumped into the pool, but Alisa got there first. Come to find out, he was faking it. By the time Alisa got to him, he had managed to lose his swim trunks. The girls would talk and laugh about this incident many times.

One night, while Alisa was working, Audrey went to a party. Audrey started feeling very uncomfortable, as in too drunk with too many male eyes on her. She called Alisa, who had just gotten off work, and asked her to come and pick her up because she had been drinking. Alisa drove 70 miles an hour on the main street to get to her. She was stopped and given a speeding ticket.

When she went to court to defend herself, she explained to the judge what happened. The judge understood and changed her moving violation to a non-moving violation. I think it was changed to a defective tail light. This ticket would not affect her driving record. He told her to be sure to slow down when saving Audrey. I was upset about the ticket but proud of how she had been faithful to Audrey. I was also proud that she was able to explain it to the judge in a calm and rational manner. She was forgiven.

When I was in the process of divorcing James, Sue and Richard had asked if they would still be able to be a part of the girls' lives. I said absolutely. I was divorcing James, not them. We agreed that the girls could visit in the summer if they wanted to. I had not had much experience with grandparents myself. Both grandfathers died before I was born, and one grandmother when I was five. The remaining grandmother was a selfish old bitch. She did not like my mother and thought Dad had made a mistake by marrying her. Mom had six kids already. Grandma needed Dad to stay on the farm. Dad was 27 when he finally left home. I felt this part of my life was missing, so I made sure the girls had access to their grandparents. But I digress.

During the summer of 2002, Debbie went to spend time with her grandparents in Ohio while Alisa and I looked for a house. We found one before Debbie returned. I think she was hurt that we did not wait to ask her opinion. (I had bought a van while in Missouri when Debbie was on another grandparent visit.) Now, when I look back, I am sure making these purchases without her input may have been detrimental to her feelings of belonging to the family.

The house had three bedrooms, two upstairs and one down on the lower level. The house was a bi-level or raised ranch; whatever you want to call it. There was a full bath upstairs and a half bath down. There was a huge family room downstairs as well. The family room was very useful over the years.

The family room served as a pool room for a while, a party room, and a place for me to set up my newly acquired long-arm quilting machine. Having made simple quilts before, I wanted to start getting into tougher designs. The quilting machine is used to attach the backing to the quilt top, where all the design is. I made many quilts over the years. Making them was stress relief for me. The girls knew if I was sewing, not to interrupt me unless they were bleeding.

Since Alisa was older, she got the bedroom in the basement. She painted the walls red and painted a black Playboy Bunny emblem over her bed. It became her haven. She was very creative with finding ways to hide her drugs. Every time she was arrested, I would clean the room from top to bottom and discover a new hiding place for her pot, along with her hollow pens and aluminum foil.

Alisa made friends quickly in the neighborhood. Her first was Jerry. She asked him if he had a blunt (joint to us old folks). He did, so they smoked together. They became very close. Jerry had a girlfriend named Katie. Over time, Katie and Jerry had a daughter, Lilly. Alisa loved that little girl. Alisa was a shoulder Katie could cry on. Jerry was getting more into drugs. He was good at fixing cars and taught Alisa some basics.

While we lived in the apartment, Debbie was in middle school at Columbia. She would ride to school with the neighbor from upstairs and then walk home. She did well in school and made quite a few friends. She started by playing the flute. She was musically inclined. She must have gotten her talent from James. I have no special musical ability. She eventually learned to play trombone, piccolo, and baritone. Her playing in band became one of the things that kept her and I bonded.

We moved into the house in early July. We were able to take our time because the lease on the apartment wasn't finished yet. Joan and Dean helped us move. We used his truck. The house was too far away from the middle school Debbie had been attending, but she wanted to finish middle school at Columbia. We figured out how to make it happen just as I had with Alisa at Legacy. I would take her to school in the morning. After school, she would walk home with her friend Shannon, where I would pick her up.

Boys were plentiful around our house. There were so many that Alisa dated that it is hard to remember. Alisa was very popular because she was beautiful and charismatic. When she walked into a room, every head would turn. She could talk to anyone and everyone about almost anything. She had many males in her life. The first few I remember were

Nate and Drew. Then came Phil. Nearly all the men in her life had some kind of a drug connection. I don't know who was dealing and who was just using, but she used right along with them. Most of these were short-term relationships; however, each was some type of abuser. Her long-term boyfriends were Heip, Brandon, Ben, and Shane. The last three, I had seen physical fights between them.

Summer was near its end. Alisa's moods were extreme, going from happy to being depressed in a short period of time. Living with her was like walking on eggshells. I felt like I was living with James again, only I couldn't divorce her.

I registered Alisa to start school at Rangeview High School for the fall semester. She enrolled in 2002 with a graduation date of 2004. Rangeview awarded her with "Most Valuable Student for May 2002." She did well in school during her sophomore year. She was building a drug network at the same time. She began to get into harder drugs rather than just smoking pot.

During the time Alisa was a sophomore, I was looking for treatment options for her condition. She hated male counselors. I did not have health insurance at the time, so we were forced to use the highly inadequate Aurora mental health system. When I called to get an appointment, I was left on hold or hung up on. When I finally did get her an appointment, she was reluctant to go. The place was utilized mostly by Medicaid recipients and court-ordered junkies. Nothing like the mental health system in Missouri.

The turnover of counselors at the clinic was very high. Almost every time I took Alisa there, she had a different counselor. She was very good at saying what the counselor wanted to hear. She did have one counselor for three visits before that counselor left. The situation was even harder because Alisa had a strong mistrust of men. She did go to a couple at the clinic, but did not really participate.

When I finally got insurance through my job, she did agree to go to see a psychiatrist, who was male. He was an older gentleman. Alisa felt she could trust him because of his age. He went on the hunt again for that magic combination of medications. The hunt was futile because Alisa was self-medicating with pot and later cocaine. Soon after she started seeing this psychiatrist, he retired. She felt abandoned. The mistrust was back.

The following August, Alisa went back to school at Rangeview as a junior. She and I were constantly butting heads. I was relieved when she wasn't home. I don't remember having a sweet sixteen party for her. Her graduation date was set for 2004, so she wanted to get her senior pictures taken. I couldn't afford a professional photographer. I was leery that Alisa would even make graduation, so Joan took the pictures on the campus of Denver University.

Alisa turned sixteen in October, so we got her permit. I warned Alisa about speeding. According to the Aurora Police blotter, Alisa was given ten speeding tickets in ten years. It doesn't sound like many, but it must be taken into consideration that she was in juvenile detention, Turning Point, Arapahoe County Jail, and New Life. She was not driving during those times.

When Alisa got her license, I bought her a pickup truck. Cheap, old truck, but seemed reliable. With keys in her hand, she was gone. She would go everywhere. She drove the truck out toward the mountains, someplace unfamiliar to me. She called to say she had blown the engine in the truck. I had to go find her. She tried to give me directions, but much of what she told me was hard to decipher. I finally found her. I don't remember the rest. I have no idea what happened to the truck.

She had seven encounters with the law between November $18^{th}$ and the new year of 2003. I called her in as a runaway three times during that same span of time. She had an assault charge, a drug possession (cocaine), larceny, and obstruction of a judicial court order. It was a busy time. I was always on edge whenever Alisa was out of the house. It was a relief not to be confronted by her, but it was just as terrifying to try to anticipate if and when she would come home, and in what condition.

Debbie and Alisa had been born just far enough apart that, except for elementary school, they were never in the same school at the same time. When the events of the next few years took place, Debbie was subjected to Alisa's actions, but not to the point of having to go to school the next day and have other students questioning her or harassing her for Alisa's actions.

Alisa was arrested at Rangeview on November 22, 2002, by Aurora Police. The charge was possession of cocaine with intent to sell. She had baggies of cocaine on her. She was taken to the Arapahoe County Jail now that she was sixteen. The case became an Arapahoe County case.

The night before she was to go to court, she went out and got high. She could not (or would not) get out of bed to go. I had to force her up and out into the car. She glared at me. She cursed at me all the way to court. It hurt, but I was determined to hold her responsible for her actions.

Alisa was assigned a public defender by the court named Peter. He became the father figure in her life that she lacked. He was stern with her about what she needed to do and made her do what she was told. At arraignment, Peter convinced the judge to release Alisa into my custody without imposing a bond.

Peter worked his magic in court and got Alisa assigned to go to a rehabilitation center for teenage girls. It was called Turning Point and located in Ft Collins. She spent much of the summer of 2003 in Fort Collins.

There, she had individual counseling, family counseling, and school. I would drive an hour and a half each way to attend the therapy sessions. I did not find them very useful. One thing that Alisa did get out of Turning Point was her GED. The center had enrolled her in a GED class at the University of Colorado, Ft Collins. She would not have to return to Rangeview. If she had stayed in school, she would not have graduated until May 2004.

She had to complete the program, which included individual therapy and family therapy. I would go to the family sessions, but James never would. His excuse was he couldn't get off work. I went to Fort Collins at least twice a week. She was angry at first about being there, but as she worked through the program, she came to a better understanding of her addiction.

The girls were counseled on their addictions, made to take classes to finish their education, plus classes that were focused on addiction itself. They were given house duties and made to get along. The girls would start with no privileges and work for the reward of having a privilege given back. Alisa kept a journal during her stay. I have added her writings to the end of this book. (The chapter is just as she wrote it, with the exception of a couple of words that I felt were too offensive.)

In addition to schoolwork and counseling, Turning Point had a psychiatrist evaluate each of the girls monthly. Alisa was taking the combination of prescriptions that had been given to her by her own psychiatrist. The psychiatrist at Turning Point told Alisa that she did not need the medication. If she was clean of street drugs, she would be fine. She was sixteen. In Colorado, a sixteen-year-old can make medical decisions for themselves. She went off her medication because of this quack at Turning Point. I could do nothing about it. I felt the system (justice and mental health) was failing her again. Everywhere I turned to get help, it was not to be found.

When Alisa finished her GED, Turning Point held a graduation ceremony. It was held outside in one of the parks in Fort Collins. I attended. I was so proud that she was now done with high school and, hopefully, her addiction. James did not attend. Alisa's public defender, Peter, was also in attendance. Then she was released since she had also completed the requirements of the program.

I don't feel that Turning Point had much of an effect on Alisa. In her Turning Point journals, she talks about leaving the facility with some other girls and partying. All the girls were under house "arrest" on the 4th of July. Basically, her journal was just a place for her to express the feelings she could not (or would not) share in therapy. It was a place where she was counting the days until release. She graduated from Turning Point in early September. The next police blotter entry is October 11, 2003, for possession of alcohol by a minor.

During the time Alisa was at Turning Point, I was working fifty or more hours a week at Kaiser Permanente as part of the team to install Epic. Epic is a completely integrated software system used to control medical encounters. There is a piece used to check people into a doctor's office. Then there is a piece for the doctor to enter information about the visit. The next piece is the billing application, which was my specialty.

I was taught how to import data and set up routines to make sure billing and collections were done correctly and in a timely manner. It is a lot more complicated than what I just described, but you get the idea.

Today, many hospitals and clinics have Epic, but I was one of the pioneers who brought Epic into the limelight. I had spent nearly a month in Madison, June 2003, to take classes on how to install the software. I would leave for Madison on Monday, be in class Tuesday through Thursday (sometimes Friday), and then come home for the weekend. Fridays, I would go to Turning Point. Debbie was at her grandparents' or her dad's house. Learning the software became a valuable asset for my future work life.

In early 2004, I decided we all needed a vacation. With system go-live in August, I asked the boss if I could take time off in March. She got angry about it and said she couldn't let me have time off with go-live six months away. I pointed out that after go-live, I would not be able to take vacation either. She finally granted me the time off, so I booked a Mexican cruise. It was only a four-day cruise. I felt the short excursion would be good for our first cruise. We would sail out of Long Beach, CA, to Catalina Island. Then, from Catalina, we went to Ensenada, Mexico.

The cruise was a mixture of fun and anger. We had an inside cabin. When we got settled in the room, Alisa said she could feel the walls closing in. Turns out she was claustrophobic. The situation was okay the first couple of days because we had port excursions.

At Catalina Island, things were good. The girls tried on dresses with a local flair. A fun game of dress-up. Then the girls wanted to go snorkeling. When they got into their wetsuits, Debbie said hers was too tight and she couldn't breathe. The tour group was able to get the suit adjusted, and Debbie was fine. They enjoyed the adventure. They were even taught facts about some of the sea life in the Pacific. It was an enjoyable day. While the girls were snorkeling, I sat in the sun, relaxing and reading a book.

Back on the ship after a day in Catalina, we headed for Ensenada. Once we arrived and deboarded the ship, we were surrounded by little kids trying to sell us beads and trinkets. It was sad to think of those kids trying to help make a living for their families. The three of us stayed together for a while. The girls had a street vendor put a poncho on their shoulders and a big floppy hat on their heads. Then he put a lizard on their shoulders, one girl at a time, so we could take pictures.

We ate at a real Mexican restaurant, where the food was delicious. Margaritas were cheap, and Alisa was close to her 18$^{th}$ birthday, so we indulged. The legal drinking age in Mexico was eighteen at the time. After eating as a family, Alisa disappeared in the crowd. She wandered around the city and got an eighteen-year-old male to buy her drinks, Coronas, I think. Alcohol was cheap, and she took advantage of it. Ten Coronas for ten dollars. I was terrified because she was out of sight in a foreign country on her own.

Debbie and I walked around seeing the sights and window shopping. I took pictures of her at some of the signs around welcoming us to Ensenada. We just enjoyed our time being alone. My worry about Alisa made it difficult to focus on Debbie, but I tried. We arrived back at the ship by the required time, and I was relieved to see Alisa had returned as well.

Dinners on the ship were structured to allow people to interact. We were placed at a table with two couples who were there for romantic reasons. We were expected to dress up for these formal dinners.

Photographers were around to take pictures. Just another way to get money out of us. As for the interaction with the other diners, that did not go very well. The food was good, and for enjoyment after dinner, there was dancing. Both girls joined the Conga line and danced away.

The last day, we could not leave the ship. It was a two-day trip back to California. No port of call to get off. Being confined to the ship was problematic for us. This was when Alisa's claustrophobia became a real problem. She was like a caged animal, cussing about how she needed to get off the ship. Knowing that she could not get off the ship, I finally let her go explore the shows and bars that were onboard. Another time, I worried about her not being with me. She would go into a bar, meet people who would buy her drinks because she looked the age. When there was no one to buy, she would move from table to table finishing off the remains of other people's drinks. She danced a lot and sang karaoke. She took pictures of the midnight buffet and then indulged in its delicious food.

I woke up about 3 A.M., and Alisa had not returned. We were scheduled to get off the ship the next morning very early. I started searching the ship for her. The ship was at least ten stories high. The search seemed daunting. I got to the top deck and found no one. I was afraid she had jumped ship or fallen overboard because I knew she was drinking.

I returned to our room to call for assistance in locating her, but she was there, passed out. I went back to bed to get a little more sleep. When it was time to deboard the ship, I had to struggle with Alisa to get dressed and finish packing. She was still drunk and belligerent. Debbie got packed and was ready to go. Alisa got angry with her as well. She was calling

Debbie names and pushing her around. I had to break it up. We had to catch the bus from Long Beach back to the airport.

Before the trip, Alisa had been on probation, which ended in February of that year. We went to Mexico in March. We were detained in customs because the computer system had not been updated and showed that Alisa was still on probation. I worried that we might never get into the country or that we would miss our flight home. Customs had to call and get the correct information. After about an hour of sitting there, we were finally allowed to move on. It was a challenge to get to the bus and back to the airport. Once we got on the plane, Alisa fell asleep. She slept the entire flight back to Denver.

After our return from Mexico, Alisa started dating a Vietnamese man named Heip. He was a little bit older than she was. I think they got together because they enjoyed playing at being a DJ. I would come home, and Alisa would be using her turntables with music blaring out the windows. She would sneak out at night through her bedroom window. I didn't hear her because her room was in the basement, in the front of the house. Mine was upstairs on the back side of the house.

Alisa and Heip were together for almost three years. While they were, she started calling herself Skittles. I did not figure it out till later; she was using that name while she was dealing or using because she did not want anyone coming to the house. She started living a secret life of drugs and dealing, and I really don't know what else. I am sure that I don't want to know.

Heip belonged to a Vietnamese gang who was into drugs, alcohol, and racing cars in town. One time, a rival gang member told police I had automatic weapons in the house. Aurora Police arrived, five cop cars strong. They came to the door and requested to search the house. The house was searched, and no guns were found. The Aurora Police became very familiar with our address.

While on a date one night, Alisa and Heip were on their way to a restaurant and saw this little dirty dog digging in a trash dumpster for food. Alisa wanted Heip to stop, but he didn't. They went on to have dinner. When dinner was over, Alisa made Heip drive back to the place where they had seen the dog. He was still there. The two of them went to different houses around to see if the dog belonged to anyone.

One neighbor told them that the dog had been owned by the people who lived in the house where he was staying. The neighbor stated the people had moved out a week ago and left the dog behind. Alisa brought the dog home. She gave him a bath and then called me to see if it was okay and could she keep him. Thus, we had a new Bichon Frise, whom she named DJ. I just called him Mutt Face. He became her best friend. She took him when she went jogging. He went everywhere with her.

I need to mention two things that I cannot put into any particular part of the timeline, but these things occurred during the years covered by this chapter. The first was a class on brain disorders. I knew what Alisa had been diagnosed with. I wanted to learn more about it and find a support group of other parents dealing with this same thing. I was able to find what I needed through Aurora Mental Health. They offered an eight-week course on disorders of the brain.

The class covered more than just bipolar disorder, which helped me learn more about the brain in general. I found the support I was looking for. One couple had adopted twins, and both children were bipolar. They were at their wits' end trying to help these kids and be a parent to them. Their families did not understand any of it. The families would ask, "Can't you just give them back?" I could feel their hurt as their situation kind of mirrored mine. I couldn't give her back, but I was judged about what kind of parent I was. I still think about that couple and wonder how things turned out for them. Alisa was very angry when she found out I had taken the class.

The other thing was, as a requirement of her probation (I don't know which one), we had to attend a program called MADRE. I think it stands for "Mothers and Daughters' Relationships." I don't think we were ever told. It didn't matter; we just had to go. The first part of the class was a joint session, then the mothers went one way, and the girls went another. In the parent portion, we learned about love and logic parenting. The class taught us how to remove the emotion from the situation. We discussed picturing our child as a stranger. Would you allow a stranger to talk to you like that? It taught de-escalation techniques. Putting what was taught into practice was hard, but it did make a difference. With this class and the brain disorder class, I felt better about myself. I felt I was more equipped to handle Alisa.

During this period, Alisa would flip back and forth with her moods. One day, she got very depressed. I took her to the emergency room for help. Since she was not bleeding or had a major physical problem, we were left in a room for about twelve hours. Alisa went from being depressed to being extremely angry. She would scream and pace, while I tried to keep her quiet. The hospital staff would come in occasionally and tell me to control my daughter. (Really?) When she was finally seen by the doctor, it was decided that she was a danger to herself and others, so they put a 72-hour hold on her, as had been done in the hospital in NY. I am glad there wasn't anything in the room that she could have attacked me or the hospital staff with.

The hospital transferred Alisa to a mental health facility in Westminster. This was about thirty miles away on the northwest side of town, near where James lived. During her stay, she was allowed to call me. She would cry and beg me to come and get her. She would tell me how horrible she was being treated. She said she had been strapped down to the bed. I wanted to rescue her, but legally, I could not. I felt guilty for having taken her to the hospital. I was finally able to take her home with instructions to get her help. (What did they think I had been doing?) Thinking about it now, I enjoyed getting some much-needed uninterrupted sleep.

I did not have insurance at the time, so I had a bill from the hospital emergency room, the emergency room doctor, the ambulance, and the mental health facility. The mental health facility alone was $7500. I contacted James about these bills, and he did not pay any of it. I had to file bankruptcy in early 2005.

Before this, I had gotten Alisa a burnt orange Grand Am for her use to get to work and school. Due to bankruptcy, that car had to be given back to the credit union where I had financed it. Alisa was livid. She ranted to me about how it was my fault that she did not have a car. I had bought my first new car ever, a 2004 maroon Grand Am. This became Alisa's car. I did not have the strength to fight with her over it. My job changed in 2008, so I was having to drive all over town. I bought a used Jeep Liberty. Alisa drove the Grand Am until it quit in the summer of 2014.

Alisa obtained her medical marijuana license. She was old enough to obtain it legally. She had a friend who was supposed to be her caregiver. She used the premise that she needed to smoke to help her sleep. I was livid. I told her that I just spent the last seven years trying to get her clean, and she runs right to it when she is old enough. I felt like I had been slapped in the face. I was so hurt; I couldn't look at her.

In May, Alisa asked if she could move out. She thought I would be mad for asking, but I was delighted. She wanted to move in with Audrey. They moved into an apartment close to Alisa's work at Blockbuster Video, so she didn't have to go far. DJ went with her. She met the neighbors, and the partying began. Then Heip moved in as well. Even though she was trying to be mature by paying her own bills and being out of the house, she continued to call me and ask for help. I do not believe she got arrested at all while she was living there. I do believe that she met a lot of people and did a lot of partying.

While Alisa lived in the apartment, I still had to take care of her to some degree. She would call me for money. One night, she called because she was scared. She had barricaded herself in the apartment. She stated she owed money to some drug dealer. She had made some kind of arrangement with whomever she owed the money to. When I arrived, she said that everything was fine. I think maybe her drug use caused her to be paranoid. This would happen a few more times as she got worse. I remember her pacing back and forth in the living room with the curtains closed. She kept mumbling that someone was coming. Thinking back, why would I go to the apartment? She was eighteen and an adult. I went because she was my sick baby.

I don't know much about her life in the apartment. She worked at Blockbuster Video. She enjoyed being on her own, even if she did have a roommate. She stayed in contact with Aurora Police. She had five entries for 2004. Two of them were for running away. One was for burglary of a residence; another was a traffic accident. The last one was victim of aggravated assault/non-family with a gun. This may have been the time she told me about staring down the barrel of a gun during a confrontation with the rival Vietnamese gang.

Alisa started taking classes to get a degree in psychology. She started at Metro State while she was living in the apartment. She was a good student. I had gone back to college when the girls were younger, so I had set an example of how important getting an education is. She was determined to finish school.

Alisa moved back home when the lease was up. She lived with me from that point on until I kicked her out on Easter of 2014. When she left to move into the apartment, the downstairs bedroom became Debbie's. Debbie and her friend Tyler painted the room blue and black. When Alisa returned the next year, she was made to take the upstairs bedroom next to mine.

Heip moved back to his parents' house at the end of the lease. I know that he spent a lot of time at our house or running around with Alisa. Once back in Aurora, Alisa changed colleges. She started attending the Community College of Aurora. The college was closer to home and her work. I believe she had quit Blockbuster and was working at Schlotzsky's (a fast-food place). The situation was better for making it to class on time. She had been late to class many times at Metro State.

Alisa and Heip started having relationship issues. They had been together nearly three years. I am not sure why they broke up. It may be in part that Heip's mother did not like Alisa because she was not Vietnamese. I remember giving a counseling session to the kids one day while they were fighting. I find that funny now, me giving relationship advice.

The fight between Alisa and Heip started at my house but moved to Heip's. His family did not live far away. His house was within walking distance of ours. I don't know what the fight was about or how I got involved. I separated the two and made them sit on the driveway to calm down. I asked Alisa if she loved him. She said yes. I asked Heip if he loved her. He said yes. I had a hard time understanding Heip at times due to his accent. I listened closely. I made each of them see the other person's point of view. I told them all couples fight, but they needed to be calm, talk things over, respect each other's feelings, and come to a compromise that was acceptable to each other.

Not long after, however, Alisa and Heip broke up. I don't know why. Maybe it was his mother's influence. Maybe they couldn't come to a compromise. I will say I had mixed feelings when they split. Alisa had always seemed happy with Heip. However, I was relieved that she would not be involved in gang violence any longer.

Alisa was a free woman again, so a string of men started coming around. One guy was Levi. He was about 6'2" and weighed about 150-180 pounds. Alisa and Levi were dating, or, more accurately, hanging out together. They had been in Alisa's bedroom (which I remember was on the main floor at that time).

When they came out, they were arguing. As they approached the stairs, Levi slapped Alisa across the face. I went momma bear on him. I was across the room in a second. I grabbed Levi by the collar and threw him down the stairs to the front door. I said, "Don't you ever hit my daughter again. You get the hell out of my house, and don't you ever come back." His face showed how stunned he was as he got up and left. I was still shaking with anger.

I believe that Levi and Alisa were dealing drugs. I don't know what kind, nor do I care. The dealing started making Alisa paranoid. She started pacing and peering out the window. I was not allowed to have the curtains open after dark. (It really didn't matter to me because I always close the curtains in the evening.) She was insistent that the blinds needed to be shut and the curtains closed. At times, Alisa was like a caged animal, pacing and darting glances everywhere.

Alisa had a friend: Jeremy. I don't know how or when Alisa met Jeremy. Alisa and Jeremy considered each other their soulmates. They hung out a lot, went to parks, and up in the mountains. Each had been in jail and on probation. They wanted to get their lives straight before they made a commitment to each other. I remember Alisa was being released from jail at 7 A.M. one morning in Arapahoe County, and Jeremy had to turn himself into Elbert County, which was more than an hour away by car. Jeremy and I picked Alisa up and drove to Elbert County Court. I drove as fast as I dared. He was supposed to be there at 9. He ran in while I parked the car. We were fifteen minutes late. He was taken to jail.

Jeremy became like a son to me. He was always respectful to me. Alisa told me not to trust him because he lied. However, he was always there for me if I needed him. He fixed the dent in the wall in the basement after Shane had thrown Alisa into it. I became like the parental figure that he had lacked growing up in South Dakota. He told me when his parents divorced, his father moved to Las Vegas. He didn't see his father much.

There was a time when his mom agreed to let him go to Vegas to spend time with his dad. He was supposed to stay a week. Jeremy said he was with his father for a day or two, and then his dad dropped him at a gas station and left. He was a teenager with no car, no money, left in the hot Las Vegas sun. He never did tell me how he got back to South Dakota. He is now in prison.

When Debbie got to high school, the band director had her start playing other instruments. She learned to play trombone. She was part of the school jazz band. During her sophomore year (early 2006), the jazz band was invited to compete in a competition in Branson, MO. It was during the week, so none of the parents could attend. I was lucky that time. I was working in Philadelphia on a contract. I was flown back and forth to Denver every week. Instead of going to Denver that weekend, I flew to Springfield, where Paula picked me up and we went to the competition. The jazz band came in first place.

Debbie learned to play baritone as well as trombone. In the marching band, she played baritone. A baritone is a brass instrument that weighs about forty pounds. I was so proud that she could play so many instruments. I was impressed with her ability to carry that instrument during performances.

The marching band competitions were held on Saturdays. Debbie would have to report to school any time between 4:30 A.M. and 6:00 A.M., depending on where the competition was located. I referred to this as zero dark thirty. I would take her to the school early for her to catch the bus to go to competition.

Many times, I would pick up other kids along the way. I got to be well-known and well-liked by the band members. When I walked in the band room after school, I had about fifty kids yell, "Hi, Mom!" These band kids helped me through the hard times when I was struggling with Alisa.

I really enjoyed going to competition even when it was freezing. Anyone who doesn't know how band competitions work, let me explain. During the summer, the kids are taught a choreographed routine to be performed on a football field. The routine is done while the kids are playing. I was always amazed at how the kids could do it. Besides remembering the music, they had to remember which direction and move to make at any one time. The Rangeview Raiders won several awards for their performances during Debbie's four years.

Alisa would tell me different things when she was mad. One night, she told me that she and Heip got into it with the other gang. She said she was staring down the barrel of a gun at one point. She was trying to keep her drug life secret, but every so often, when she wanted to get her way, she would inject into our conversation something that she had been involved with that she knew would upset me.

During this time Alisa was raped by a neighbor boy. He broke in the house through the deck window and raped her while I was working. She didn't tell me for a long time. Months or years later. When she did, I tried to get her press charges, but she refused. She told me before her death that the boy had apologized to her. The apology was enough for her, but not me. I know that this incident had to affect Alisa's mental state, which was already fragile enough.

Denver has red light cameras. Alisa would get tickets for running red lights. The car was registered in my name, so I would make a copy of my driver's license and send it in. The picture from the camera was a tall, skinny blonde, but the license showed an older lady with dark hair and overweight. I know we cheated the system that way. There were so many other issues to deal with every day that her barely running a red light was low on the priority list.

Debbie's friends planned a surprise sweet sixteen birthday party for her. She turned sixteen in February of 2005. The friends came over and decorated the basement while Debbie was out. She came home and was very pleasantly surprised.

The enjoyment of the party did not last long. It lasted until Alisa came home. Alisa's room was the basement room at the time. I told her that Debbie was having a party, and please don't do anything to disrupt it. However, Alisa proceeded to run downstairs and drop her pants, so she mooned Debbie's party. Debbie yelled upstairs to tell me what happened. Alisa was coming back upstairs laughing. I chewed her out, but she just laughed and left again.

I was offered a job as a consultant in January of 2006, which would require me to be out of town four days a week. This new opportunity was the result of all the hard work at Kaiser. The jobs always came with large salaries due to the concessions I had to make. I was an Epic Resolute Professional Billing Analyst. All those classes in Madison had paid off. I became one of the most respected analysts in the country. Over twelve years, I worked at Children's of Philadelphia, Children's of Boston, Duke University, the University of Nebraska, and several others.

I struggled with the decision about taking the job, so we had a family meeting to talk it out. The money was great, but I would miss Debbie's senior year of high school. Debbie was a junior in high school, and Alisa was in college and working. As we talked it out, Debbie was adamant that I take the job. She stated that this was the opportunity I had worked so hard for by going back to college. She did not want to stand in my way. Alisa was fine with it. Life on the road would be hard. I thought I wouldn't be playing referee to the girls any longer.

There is a police blotter entry from January 13, 2006. It states Alisa was a victim of an assault. I know she never told me about it. She knew I would give up consulting and find a job in Denver again.

A neighbor and friend, Jeff, lived two doors up. He was a single father with two boys to raise. I had helped him out over the years, picking up or taking his boys to hockey practice. His oldest son, Tyler, spent a lot of time with Debbie. When I started traveling, Jeff agreed to keep an eye on the girls, and if they needed anything, they would ask him. He had to break up many fights when the girls' fights would come out into the street. Occasionally, one or the other would call James.

The stress of being a "Road Warrior" soon became apparent. I had to make travel arrangements, including flights, hotels, and rental cars (if allowed). I used my American Express for the business expenses. I had to turn in time sheets every week, along with receipts for travel. Some assignments would reimburse only what you spent on food, while others would give a day-to-day rate that you were limited to. I always liked the per diem ones.

I never spent much on food, so the extra money was good. One contract had a per diem amount of $50 a day. I couldn't eat that much food in a day. I usually spent $20-$30 a day.

Most clients had arrangements with certain hotels to give a discounted rate to the consultants working at their site. Some of the clients did not. They would give a per-night rate that we had to adhere to, such as no more than $150 for hotel. They didn't care where you stayed as long as you were compliant with the cap. If you went over, it was not reimbursed.

I was off to Philadelphia. A typical consultant's schedule was usually to fly into the site Monday morning, work until Thursday afternoon, and then fly home. I did not adhere to this schedule. My standard was that the client needed me to be present and fully functioning on Monday morning. This meant leaving Sunday afternoon from Denver to arrive in Philly (or wherever) around midnight or later. I would then catch a shuttle to the hotel. I got to be friends with the shuttle driver. I have a lot of admiration for shuttle drivers, hotel staff, and restaurant servers.

They take a lot of crap from travelers. (Next time you travel, please be nice to these people.)

Besides having to make arrangements, keep receipts and time sheets, some clients wanted a status report every week. This had to be done on your own time. The actual travel itself was stressful. At first, I got stuck in the middle seat on the plane, or would get someone who talked the whole way. I just wanted to be left alone with my thoughts. Getting on the plane in the later boarding groups meant you may not have a bin space for your carry-on, too. As I earned status with the airlines, I was able to move into higher boarding groups. With Frontier Airlines, I was able to board first because I was an elite traveler.

I would often get phone calls at night from one or the other daughter about something. The girls would forget about the two-hour time difference. I would try to go to bed at 10 EST, which is 8 MST. The calls would come after 10. Sometimes I would be on the phone for an hour or more. It made me feel guilty for leaving them. They would always ask if I could call the other and talk to them, so I had to play referee from Philadelphia. However, I did see this as an opportunity to wean the girls off their dependency on me. I had hopes of them learning to fight their own battles. Eventually, it did. The entire first month in Philly, I cried myself to sleep every night.

One night, Debbie called James to break up another fight. When he arrived, he and Alisa got into a verbal argument in the street. Then she took off. James called me to get in touch with Alisa and make her come home so he could discipline her. I had to explain to him that she was not coming home until he left. James left, and Alisa returned home. That night, I was the referee to all three.

I stated above that the job provided substantial compensation. I finally felt financially comfortable, but along with that came the perks. I got to keep my award miles from the airlines, my hotel points, and free rental car days. We used the perks to take free vacations and reconnect with each other.

In the fall of 2006, I was able to take some time off, so we took our second vacation. We flew to Atlanta and drove to Hilton Head Island. We used my frequent flyer miles and hotel points. The only cost was for the activities we wanted to do. This was basically a free trip.

This trip was so relaxing compared to our Mexican cruise. The girls got along pretty well. Alisa was in one of her more positive moods the whole time. We played miniature golf. Each of us overshot the holes by at least two strokes. We laughed. We went kayaking. Each girl got their own boat, but since I am afraid of water and have no upper-body strength, I got in the two-person kayak with the trip master. The channel out to the bay was very calm. I tried hard, but never did get the hang of how to move the boat forward.

Later that day, we took an afternoon cruise around the bay. It was just us and the driver. As we were floating around, the dolphins came in for dinner. That was interesting. As the evening tide comes in, the dolphins chase the fish up onto the sandy bank among the reeds and eat them. I knew that dolphins ate fish, but I was not aware that dolphins hunted them as well. The experience was quite a sight to see.

Alisa's mood stayed consistent that week. We took a day and drove into Savannah, GA. The town is quaint with hanging moss and a village square at each intersection. We strolled around the historical places and took pictures. Alisa went down to the water's edge alone. I worried a bit, but not like I had at other times. She was twenty at the time. If she got into trouble, she would have to bear the consequences. Debbie and I continued to enjoy the sights.

When Alisa returned, we joined a group to take a walking ghost tour. There were a lot of stories to be told. Many of the stories were about women who stayed on shore while their husbands worked on fishing vessels at sea. I remember one about a woman who watched from the widow's peak of her house endlessly, but her husband never returned. She died in the house and is known to be seen up at the widow's peak to this day.

Not to leave the men of Savannah out, one story told of a fisherman who came home to find his girl off with another man. He proceeded to murder both of them. Their ghosts haunt the town looking for each other.

I chalked this trip up as a success. I don't remember any major confrontations with Alisa or any mood swings. She would occasionally say something to annoy Debbie, but what set of siblings doesn't get on each other's nerves sometimes? I did enjoy the trip overall.

When we returned, a new man entered the scene. Ben was a commercial roofing contractor who came to Colorado to work. At that time, Alisa was working at Bono's BBQ. The restaurant was right near the hotel where Ben was staying. He would eat dinner there. He and Alisa started dating. Again, a man who abused her. He moved in with us. Between jobs, he would go back to Iowa. During one of those times, Alisa took her first solo road trip to Iowa to see him. She was out of my sight, alone on Interstate 80 driving through sparsely populated corn and wheat fields. I did not sleep until she returned. That relationship lasted about a year, until Ben's work in Colorado was done.

The remainder of 2006 was pretty uneventful. It appears Alisa was pulled over by Aurora Police for a non-moving traffic violation in December. Only a non-moving traffic stop was no big deal by that time. Another year closer to being an empty nester.

# CHAPTER ELEVEN

## *2007-2014*

The following year (2007) started off horribly with the house being robbed while I was in Philadelphia. At least two people were involved, but it was never determined who those people were. Most of the items stolen were from Alisa. She was missing her laptop, CDs, movies, and jewelry. I didn't know if there were any drugs in the house, but if there were, I'm sure they were stolen as well. I had costume jewelry stolen as well as a ring my father had given me when my divorce was final. It was heart-shaped with a garnet (my birthstone) and a small diamond. Losing the ring was devastating to me. In my heart, I knew that it wasn't Dad's idea, but I pretended it was. The rest were just cheap necklaces and rings. There was a rather large cubic zirconia diamond ring, which wasn't worth anything. I would like to have seen the thieves' faces when they tried to pawn it. I felt the robbery was related to whatever Alisa was into at the time.

In February, James tried to commit suicide after his second wife told him she wanted a divorce. He was in the hospital for a week, which included Debbie's birthday. When there was no contact with her on her birthday, she was very upset. I felt that he had forgotten her birthday just as he had forgotten my birthday. My heart hurt for her. None of us knew anything about what was happening. While in the hospital, James was treated for his mental illness, which was the first time he admitted to anyone but me that he needed help. I was working fifty percent remote during this time, so I was able to be present for Debbie. I did what I could to ease the pain, but I know it didn't help.

After James recovered and became more stable from the medication he was given, he decided to tell the girls about what he had done. He felt they should know, just as he had thought they should meet every one of his dates/girlfriends.

He invited Debbie first to go to dinner with him. Debbie thought it was her birthday dinner. She was horrified when James proceeded to tell her how he had slit his wrists and was bleeding out on the floor. He even showed her the bandages on his wrists. At the last possible moment, he dialed 911. The paramedics had to break down the door to save him. He said the reason he called was because he wanted to be there to walk her down the aisle on her wedding day. She came home crying and visibly shaken. She told me what had happened. I was furious. How could he do something like that? Not only the actual act, but then to spell it out in detail for his daughter.

Then it was Alisa's turn. She was so excited to go have dinner with Dad. Excitement turned to shock as James started to tell his story. Alisa bolted from the restaurant to her car, crying. She sat and cried for a while, then got angry. She drove to find something to help her cope. She found a meth dealer and got high. I was fearful when she didn't come home until late. I didn't know what to do or how to help her cope. I am still angry with James about his choice to share his adventure with the girls. I blame him for Alisa's death. If he had kept his mouth shut, maybe I could have gotten her help.

Alisa was back to drugs. She was arrested on April 1 for possession of a controlled substance with intent to distribute. She had cocaine and meth on her. This case was transferred to Arapahoe County. I don't know how she got back on the street after this arrest. I did not help her.

By May she was addicted to meth. This was the only time she ever admitted to me that she had a drug problem. She told me over the phone, so I told her we would figure it out. Before we could do anything, Alisa was arrested for possession by Arapahoe County Sheriff. I was relieved when I heard she was in jail. She would not have access to drugs, and I could breathe for a while.

I was still working in Philadelphia during that time. It was my first assignment as a contractor. The contract was to be for a year. At the end of that year, the hospital wanted me to stay on. I told them I would if I could work from home every other week. They agreed. This allowed me to focus on getting Debbie through graduation and trying to get through to Alisa.

The only time Debbie really was a problem in high school was her senior year. She started dating a guy named Chad. I did not like him. Chad brought out the rebellious side of Debbie. Debbie had never done drugs or drank in high school, but she did start smoking. I found this strange because her dad was a smoker, and she was always after him to quit. Chad was abusive. He was verbally abusive at first. Then I heard about him pushing her into a brick wall outside the school.

When I arrived back in Denver, Debbie and I had a fight. She kept saying she was going to leave and go to Chad's. It was near midnight, and she was going to walk. It wasn't that far, but I was stern about her not walking alone through the neighborhood at that late hour. I'm not sure if Chad came to pick her up, but she did get to his house that night. Maybe I took her. She called later and asked me to pick her up.

Prom was coming up, and Debbie asked to go with Chad. I said no. She was eighteen. I was an absentee parent because of work, so she and her friends decided they would go behind my back. Debbie told me she was going to the prom with Nate, who was gay. She spent the evening with Chad. I found out later.

Finally, after a few months of being with Chad, Debbie decided she needed to get out. I remember the situation got ugly. Chad did not take the breakup well at all. After Debbie broke up with him, he started rumors at school that she was a slut. He would taunt her at school. His friends would do the same. It was close to the end of Debbie's high school years, which made it easier on her than having to deal with it again in the fall. Debbie met Nick not long after she graduated. Nick helped keep Chad at bay.

I came home from work one week to find Nick living with us. No one had bothered to ask me. He was having issues with his parents at the time. His mother would call him many times a day. Him living with us caused me heartache. When he moved in, he had very few clothes, and those were hand-me-downs from his brother Tom. Tom was quite a bit larger than Nick, so those clothes were way too big.

I was paying the mortgage and all the bills. Now, I started buying extra food for Nick and Debbie. I bought Nick clothes. Eventually, they convinced me to cosign a car loan for Nick. What a mistake that was. The car was a Chevy Cobalt with payments less than $200 a month. Nick would pay sometimes, but most of the time, it was up to me. I tried repossessing it, but that made the chasm between myself and Debbie even worse. In the end, I sold the car to a friend of mine.

While Debbie was finishing her senior year, Alisa was getting deeper into trouble. Debbie was set to graduate, not only from high school but from college as well. She had taken an automotive class at Pickens Technical College. It is a vocational school. Her graduation ceremonies were on back-to-back nights in mid-May. Alisa was arrested about a week before Debbie was to graduate. I was upset that she had been arrested for methamphetamine possession, but relieved at the same time. She would be incarcerated when Debbie's ceremonies were being held. We could have a nice graduation party without any drama.

Even though Debbie was graduating from college the night before, she graduated from high school, we had one graduation party. We decorated the house in Rangeview Raider red and black. Debbie invited several classmates. The party was well attended. I made hamburgers for all and provided chips and sodas. The kids played volleyball in the backyard. Many just sat on the deck and joked around. It was a good day. I was so proud of her.

Debbie decided to take a year off before getting into any type of secondary education. She really could not make up her mind what she wanted to do with her life. She thought about auto mechanics, since she had taken the class at Pickens Tech. She also thought about being a massage therapist so she could work at the resorts in the mountains. There were a couple of other ideas, but these two were the biggest contenders. During the time she was deciding, she worked at Domino's and then Jimmy John's.

After Debbie's graduation, I went back to focusing on Alisa. She was in jail and was trying to get me to bail her out. Again, I would not. She was in real jail now. In order to visit her, I had to drive approximately thirty minutes each way. I was allowed a thirty-minute visit. During the visit, we talked on the phone, and we could see each other on closed-circuit TV.

I hired a lawyer by putting down a $1500 retainer fee. The lawyer and I started talking about a strategy that would be best for Alisa. The lawyer wanted to leave her in jail, which I agreed with, until a slot became available at the Arapahoe House. Arapahoe House is a drug and alcohol rehabilitation facility where many court cases were sent. He said a thirty-day outpatient treatment center would be sufficient. I asked how long until a spot would become available. He said it could take up to a year for her to be admitted into the program. I was livid. An outpatient treatment program was in no way going to cure her addiction. I fired him. When I hired him, he said any unused funds that I had paid would be refunded. I asked for a refund. He sent me a statement showing charges equal to what I had paid. Again, I was livid. What an ass he was.

I went to find Peter again. He had done such a great job with Alisa when she was arrested at Rangeview. By this time, Peter was a magistrate for Adams County courts. He could no longer represent Alisa. He gave me Darrin's name and number. Darrin was a Godsend for me. Darrin agreed that Alisa needed professional help. We agreed that Arapahoe House was not the place. He came up with a plan he thought the court would consider. We would send Alisa to an out-of-state rehabilitation facility for the extensive treatment she needed.

Darrin met with Alisa to outline the plan. She gladly agreed to it. She was finally ready to kick her life of addiction. She wanted to learn how to control her bipolar disorder. She wanted to be normal.

I started researching facilities. Darrin had recommended one in Arizona, but it was way more than I could afford. I kept looking until I found New Life in San Francisco. The program lasted five or more months, depending on the patient. The cost was $15,000. I had to take out a second mortgage on the house and borrow against my life insurance policy to come up with the money. James certainly was not going to help with the cost. He had stated that she was my problem. Technically, she wasn't even my problem since she was twenty years old.

Alisa remained in jail until her court date. Darrin presented the plan, and thankfully, the judge agreed with it. I think he agreed, in part, because Alisa had been in his court at least twice before. I called New Life to arrange an admission date. They said they could take her on July 5th. Having been arrested in May, Alisa was in jail for about six weeks. The judge agreed to let her out of jail on the 4th of July so she could have one day at home before leaving. I brought her home for the day.

The following morning, I took Alisa to the airport to catch her flight to San Francisco. I could not walk to the gate with her due to extra security having been put in place after 9-11. New Life was to pick her up and take her to the facility. I worried when she got out of sight that she wouldn't get on the plane or would leave the San Francisco airport before she could be picked up. I finally got a call from her saying she was at her new home. I felt a major weight being lifted from my shoulders. I took a deep breath and relaxed for the first time in months.

The program at New Life was very strict. I couldn't have any contact with Alisa for the first month she was there. During that first month, she was put on a healthy diet and exercise program. She was also required to sit in the sauna for a certain amount of time each day. This was to detoxify her body. She told me that she could smell the drugs coming out of her pores.

Alisa was finally able to call. I was so happy to hear her voice. She explained that she had been in detox. In addition to the daily sauna, she was taking various vitamins, eating healthy, spending time going to the gym, and taking classes. She said it was amazing to her that the smell of marijuana and the other drugs was still very strong. She had expected they would be gone due to her length of time in jail. I was surprised too at first. I thought about how long she had been doing drugs, and then it made sense.

She became part of a support group with other patients who had similar issues. New Life focused on total mind and body cohesiveness. The group was allowed to go out together to see the city. They went to the gym nearly every day. Brandon was in charge. He was near the end of his program, so he was empowered to take on the challenge of seeing the others to the gym and back.

The group was allowed to take a trip to see the San Francisco Giants play baseball. Alisa's favorite place to go in San Francisco was the Japanese Tea Garden. It is so quiet and peaceful there.

I was allowed to visit her after the initial intake. I flew to San Francisco to see just how much better she was. She had gained weight and had more color. She had been taught how to use the public transportation system, so we took busses to the Japanese Tea Garden. The tea garden is so serene that it just sinks into your heart and soul. We both felt at peace. She was very happy. I was happy too. I loved her so much and was proud of the progress she was making.

Alisa's program was scheduled to end in November. She worked really hard and was given many awards for completing different aspects of the program. One of the requirements of the program was to make amends to the people she had hurt. She had always made nasty remarks about my faith in God. During the last few weeks of her stay, she was required to call me and apologize for all the things she had said about my faith. After the call, I felt such a relief. I felt pride in my ability to have continued being strong in faith even throughout everything she had put me through.

Her 21st birthday was coming. I asked if she thought she could come home for that weekend. She had doubts but asked anyway. Being that close to finishing the program, she was allowed time off to come home. We had a small family get-together at the house, including Sue and Richard. I can see her sitting at the end of the table, enjoying her time home.

Before the get-together was over, Sue had to tell us about Alisa's Aunt Pat, dying of ovarian cancer, in September. She did so in an offhanded kind of way. I think she took that approach because Pat didn't belong to her, just Richard. Sue and Richard used to take the girls to Pat's house every so often so Debbie and Alisa could get to know Pat and her family. Alisa and Debbie both had a connection to Pat. Her sons were older, but when the girls would go to their house, the boys doted on them. Hearing that Aunt Pat had passed away, Alisa became quite upset. She excused herself and went out on the deck to smoke a cigarette. I was so disgusted by the way Sue had handled the news, I wanted to strangle her. How can you give bad news like that to a recovering addict who has not even completed rehab? She returned to San Francisco and completed the program with success.

When Alisa returned home from New Life, she brought one of the other people who had been in New Life with her: Brandon. He had completed his program. He and Alisa had fallen in love. I have several pictures of him and Alisa. She looked so happy. He really seemed to treat Alisa right. He took her to Las Vegas to meet his parents. After a while, he started using again. He and Alisa began fighting. Last I knew, he was headed to Wyoming to find work.

When there was a downturn in the economy in 2008, I was let go from the assignment I was on. There were no new consulting positions to be found. The consulting company paid me for a while, even though I wasn't actively working. This is called "bench" time. It only lasted a couple of months. I knew I had to get a regular job.

I applied at the Children's Hospital of Denver and was hired on. Epic was working with the federal government to subsidize doctors' offices to get the electronic medical record. Children's created a specialized team, including me, to come up with a downsized version of the software that could be installed in the doctors' offices while utilizing the hospital's base system. It was a new idea back then, but now it is commonplace. The program was quite successful. The roll-out of the software to our first doctor's office happened within about eighteen months. We had three more doctors who wanted to sign on as well. I worked there for about two years until the economy recovered.

I still had reward points for Marriott, Frontier, and Enterprise, so it was time for another vacation. Our vacations were usually to some place warm, and most of the time included a beach. However, in the summer of 2008, we headed for Alaska. I had disclosed to the girls where we were going. Debbie was okay with it. Alisa, on the other hand, was appalled. I told her she didn't have to go. After taking some time to get used to the idea, she came around and decided she wanted to go too.

Our trip was scheduled for June, and I only had a couple of days of vacation I could use, so it was going to be a short trip. I had enough rewards to stay four days. Being a mountain girl, I had always wanted to see Mount McKinley. We flew from Denver to Anchorage. We spent our first night in a Marriott hotel. We checked into the hotel and went to find dinner. We arrived around 10 P.M., but the sun was still up. We did not realize what time it was because the sun seemed to be setting. We tried several places to eat, only to find each restaurant closed. It finally occurred to us that it was past midnight. I think we ended up with fast food that night.

The next morning, we boarded a train for Denali National Forest. The train went through a few small towns, including Wasilla. As we passed by certain points of interest, the conductor would point them out. I found it interesting passing the petrified forest. These trees were affected by an earthquake measuring 9.2 on the Richter scale, which happened in March of 1964. The conductor explained how the trees ended up looking like they do, but I can't remember. I think the petrification was due to the amount of saltwater the trees had taken in.

Continuing on, we discovered many people had planes in their backyards. The planes seem to be almost as common as a car would be in the lower 48. The explanation was that Alaska is so remote in some areas that planes are the only way in and out. Debbie and I watched for wildlife. We saw a moose and some beautiful swans. Alisa slept pretty much the whole way. That was okay.

The train trip was about six hours long, I think. We had dinner on the train. The meal was included in the train fare. I enjoyed the scenery and took lots of pictures of trees, mountains, and the Eagle River. We arrived at the base of Mt. McKinley. I had arranged to spend the night in a cabin near the river. The cabin was cozy. Not very big with two queen-size beds. I crawled into bed and fell asleep quickly. Alisa and Debbie went in and out of the cabin a couple of times to smoke.

Morning came. We rose and packed up. We would not be returning to the cabin. On the itinerary was a back-country jeep excursion. We were magically transported from the cabins to the location of the jeep tour office. (I say magically because I really don't remember how we got there. I didn't have a rental car.) At the office, we met with the crew leader and was shown our jeep. Both girls, of course, wanted to drive. I was afraid of an argument. It was avoided because no one under 25 could drive the jeep. I was happy and excited to do so. I had been four-wheeling with James and had been terrified. This time, I was in control.

The tour started with everyone getting lined up and checked for seatbelts. Alisa thought the tour guide was cute. We had a CB radio, which Alisa used to keep in touch with the leader. Debbie was in the back filming. I expected the road to be rough, but it exceeded my expectations. We went through mud puddles that were larger in diameter than the jeep itself. One puddle was so deep that the water came up to the bottom of the jeep. With the girls cheering me on, I drove through like a champ. I was glad Debbie was taping. Now I could watch myself drive through the puddle.

We ended the forward trek at a campsite set up in the wilderness. The leader told us to stay in our jeeps when we arrived so the camp could be checked out for bears. When all was clear, the guide and a cook, who was at the campsite, made us a great meal of beef stew. Finishing the adventure meant we had to go back the way we came. The trip wasn't as exciting going back since we knew what to expect.

Upon returning to the office, we were once again magically transported back to the train for the ride back to Anchorage. We spent the last day in Anchorage seeing the sights and, of course, shopping. Returning to the airport, a minor incident happened. It seemed huge at the time because we were all tired. I don't remember what happened, but I do remember being angry with both girls. I had gotten us checked in, then they went outside to have a smoke. I went out to join them in the warm sun. I was very angry, so I asked Alisa for a cigarette. The girls just looked at me like I had two heads. Debbie said, "Mom, you don't smoke." I said, "Today I do. If you two are going to smoke and fight, I'm going to smoke." I am not sure what effect it had on the girls, but I wanted to show them I wasn't taking any more. After that, the flight home was uneventful. This turned out to be another enjoyable trip overall.

Life went back to normal with the feeling of walking on eggshells when I was home. One night, Alisa and Debbie were fighting. I tried to break it up. Alisa kicked me in the abdomen with intense force. She was high. Debbie called the police, but Alisa left before they could arrive. Alisa later apologized to Debbie, saying she did not remember any of it.

Debbie had made her decision about what she wanted to do with her life. She wanted to be a massage therapist. She started a year-long program in the fall of 2008. She was taking classes and started working at Check into Cash. Many times, she would not get out of work soon enough to get to class on time. When the second half of the program started, she stopped going. She said the school was just repeating what she had already learned. Without the motivation to continue and working so many hours, she quit school.

Alisa started dating Shane. He was a bum with epilepsy. He lived with his mother in Pueblo and was on disability (I think). He had a medical marijuana license to smoke pot for his condition. When he purchased the pot, he would get enough so Alisa could smoke too. He was into other drugs as well. He was abusive to Alisa.

I don't know how the two met, but he was soon coming around. Alisa would travel to Pueblo to see him. Pueblo is about one hundred miles from Aurora. She would stay down there with DJ. She and Shane would take DJ to the park with a stream running through it. They would put him in a plastic tub so he could float down the stream. Alisa told me about Shane's mother. She was a doped-out hippie and would drink, smoke pot, and dance around her courtyard without a care in the world.

Alisa was working as a server, so being in Pueblo was not working out for her. The two moved into my house. I would buy groceries while I was home, and the cabinets would be empty when I got home. There was no financial contribution from either of them. Just as with Ben, the two argued a lot. I would tell them to leave, so they would just go out front and continue fighting in the street. Neighbors would call the police. When police arrived, Shane would be faking a seizure. Alisa was made to look like the aggressor, not the victim. She was arrested one time for domestic abuse.

I came home one Thursday night to find a huge dent in the wall in the basement. It was shaped like a human body. I asked Alisa what happened. She said that it was an accident. I knew it wasn't, but was too tired to fight about it. I just put it on the list of things to be repaired. I told Alisa that Shane needed to move out. My friend Elaine had a camper for sale, so Shane bought it. It was placed in my backyard so Shane could still be close.

Near the end of their relationship, Shane arranged to have the trailer moved to Pueblo near his mother. Shane broke into the house and stole two laptops, mine and Alisa's. Thankfully, he did not steal my work laptop. That is how we knew it was him. Anyone else would have taken all three laptops. Shane knew which one was my personal machine. Both my work and personal laptops sat on my desk, right next to each other. Only one disappeared.

Alisa had damning information on her laptop that could be used against him. We thought he took mine as well, in case Alisa had given me a copy of the information. I'm not sure if we filed a police report, and I don't remember getting the insurance company involved. I did get a restraining order towards Shane after the relationship was over.

Debbie and Nick moved into an apartment for a year in 2009. They had trouble managing money, so at the end of lease they moved back home, June 2010. The house got pretty crowded sometimes. Alisa, DJ, Nick, Debbie, and Rusty (Debbie's dog). It was hard on all of us, even though I was still on the road and out of town four days a week. I was in Sacramento then.

Debbie and Alisa would still fight, but with Nick there, I got calls much less often. I would come home and go grocery shopping, then leave again. Thursdays, I would return home to dirty dishes in the sink. (We had a dishwasher.) The fridge and cabinets would be empty. I didn't mind the empty cabinets, but the dirty dishes pissed me off. Debbie would say they were Alisa's dishes. I would start cleaning up, then Debbie would get mad. She said it made her feel like she wasn't doing enough around the house.

Nick asked me for Debbie's hand in marriage. I said okay. Nick was still a teenager, but I saw him as having potential. I saw him as Aladdin, a diamond in the rough. I could see how much he loved her. They set a date of July 17, 2011. Debbie started planning. I gave her a budget of $5000 with no more than $500 for a dress.

I wanted to start investing for my retirement. The time was good for buying property. It was a buyer's market. Lots of inventory but few buyers. Many homes were in foreclosure. I wanted to take advantage of these economic conditions. I started looking at condominiums to purchase as a rental property.

I found a couple of condos that I could afford. Debbie and Nick jokingly asked if I was buying it for them to live in. I did want them out of my house. The two of them had bad credit, so we started discussing this purchase more seriously. I decided to put Nick as the primary owner with me as the cosigner. We felt that this was a good way to improve Nick's credit score to help them in the future. I regretted this decision many times afterward.

The agreement was, they would pay the mortgage, and I would pay the HOA fees. We purchased the condo in January 2011. They had moved in, and we had remodeled with new paint and carpet. They made one payment. I had stated when it came time to file taxes, I was going to take the interest on the mortgage as a deduction. When I told the kids, they decided to stop paying. They looked at the situation like I was stealing from them. To keep my credit in good standing, I started paying the mortgage and the homeowners' association fees.

It turned out the lady who lived next door was a troublemaker. The person who had owned the condo before us had been an older lady who was always quiet. She had passed away. The condo was on the market to settle the estate. We did not do our due diligence in checking the neighborhood. Anyway, before the first month was up, Peggy was calling the cops on the kids for being too loud. Police would come, but the sound was never that loud. The cop would sit in the turnaround in front of the place and listen. Most of the time, the noise level was acceptable.

Peggy did not like having a young couple living next door, so when she couldn't get them for disturbing the peace, her next move was to complain about the parking situation. Each condo had a driveway and a garage. Nick would have friends over, only for Peggy to complain that the guests were blocking her driveway.

The kids all smoked. Debbie, Nick, and all their friends. At that time, they only smoked cigarettes. They did not smoke in the house. They all smoked in the garage. That became Peggy's next complaint. She could smell the smoke in her condo. She also complained there was way too much noise in the garage. She probably called the police on Debbie and Nick at least once a week that first year.

The condo had air conditioning. Unfortunately, the system was not strong enough to cool the upstairs. I got a free-standing portable air-conditioning unit from a friend of mine to use in the bedroom upstairs. It had a hose that needed to be out the window. Nick hooked it up, and they began using it. Boy, did Peggy go off that time. She called the cops because she smelled pot smoke coming from the unit. Police came and searched the premises. They found nothing.

Eventually, the kids and I talked about switching houses. Since I was on the road a lot, Peggy could have her peace. The kids would have more room for their friends without being turned into police all the time. Another option we discussed was Alisa moving into the condo. She had been so angry that I was "buying" Debbie and Nick a house. She thought I should buy one for her also.

Besides calling the police, Peggy would call the homeowners' association. She was trying to get us out of the place. We owned the place for four and a half years. Peggy continued her harassment for the entire four years. It got so bad that she started complaining to the HOA. Nick started getting letters reminding him of the HOA standards. It finally got to the point where the HOA told us we had to settle the disagreement in court or through mediation.

Debbie and Nick were to be married in July of 2011. Debbie did most of the planning with the help of her friends. The venue was a cute little chapel on the west side of town. The colors for the wedding were teal and black. These are the colors of Nick's favorite football team, the Philadelphia Eagles. Alisa was the maid of honor. Her dress was solid black. There were four bridesmaids and ushers. Nick's friend CJ was the best man. The girls were in teal green with black sashes. The guys were in black with teal ties.

James and I split the cost to a degree. It wasn't a fifty-fifty split, but close. Debbie and I had gotten everything arranged except the food. Nick's Aunt Beth was going to make the cake. The photographer was a friend of theirs. We were in the process of finding a catering company when I got a call that my mother was sick.

I had been to see Mom during the middle part of June, and she seemed fine. It was the last week of June when she got sick. She was mixing her medications up. She was refusing to go to the hospital because she said she didn't want to die in the hospital. Before she would get in the ambulance, she made everyone agree that she would be brought back home. She was taken to the hospital by ambulance and admitted. She was too sick and unstable to return home that night. She was diagnosed with sepsis, which is a blood infection.

Mom was put on antibiotics and fluids to replenish her body. Paula came to help. Henry and Carol had been taking care of Mom at home. Members of the family would fight in the hospital over what should be done for her. I was not there yet, so I can't say for sure what happened. Amber (niece) said Mom called her one day because the nurses weren't answering her call button. Amber drove from her house to the hospital, which took about thirty minutes, to find Mom's call button was still on. Amber got Mom cleaned up and settled back in bed.

I was scared about losing Mom. I felt helpless since I was so far away. I was working in Sacramento during this time. The family tried to keep me in the loop. Carol or Paula would call with updates on her condition. I guess things got ugly at the hospital among family members. I'm glad I wasn't there. It was hard enough knowing Mom was dying. I don't think I could have handled family members accusing each other of trying to run Mom's life. Carol had been Mom's primary caregiver. She had done a great job.

Finally, everyone left the hospital. When Mom was stabilized, the ambulance took her back to her house. The bed was in the living room, like Dad's had been.

Family members came and went. Henry and Carol kept the vigil going. Henry was with her when she passed. It had been only four hours from when the ambulance brought her home until her final breath. Henry had been trying to encourage her to hang on because I was on my way. She did not make it. She died while we were in flight.

I don't remember the exact timing, but I think Mom got sick early in the week at the end of June. Being in Sacramento, I had a long way to fly. I arranged for flights into Philadelphia for the four of us—me, the girls, and Nick. We took a rental car to drive the four hours home. As we landed in Philadelphia, we got the news that Mom was gone. It was no hurry to get upstate NY now, so we took our time. We all sat in silence during the trip. We checked into the hotel in Binghamton to get some sleep.

Mom died early morning, July 3rd, 2011. It was a Sunday. The coroner came to do his duty, and then Mom was taken from the house. Because Monday was a holiday, we could not make plans with the funeral home until Tuesday. Mom wanted to be cremated and had left instructions about her service. She would be placed in the plot with Dad. She had also written goodbye letters to each of us.

Paula and Ralph took control of planning things. Paula was Mom's executor, so it was expected she would do most of the planning. She told me to meet the family at 3:30 at the funeral home. The four of us got started on the drive from Binghamton to be there on time. During the trip, Allyssa (niece) called saying Paula had moved the time from 3:30 to 4 P.M. We had time to waste with the extra half-hour, so we went to Mom's house.

I received a call from Adam about 3:40 asking where I was. I said at Mom's. Adam was upset because they had already started planning the funeral at 3:30, just like originally planned. We rushed over to find Adam outside smoking, visibly upset. He asked why we were late. I told him about Allyssa's call.

Alisa and I went in to see everyone gathered around the table with Paula and Ralph at the head, obviously in charge. There was a seat next to Paula, so I moved to sit down. Alisa stayed at the door. Paula made a nasty remark to me. I don't remember about what, but Alisa let her in, saying she couldn't talk to me like that. Paula's comeback: "You shouldn't even be here!" Alisa stormed out.

The service was planned using Mom's instructions. The letters were given out. We parted ways, with me and my girls heading back to Mom's house. When we arrived, we found that the house had been stripped of nearly everything. I was angry that the family had descended like vultures. As I looked around, I said, "Well, I got everything I wanted from Mom. I got her looks and determination. I don't need any physical things."

I wasn't sure I wanted to read my letter. I knew in my heart that Dad saw me as just another mouth to feed, and Mom always covered for him. I was afraid she would tell me that it was all my imagination. I read the letter when we returned to the hotel for the night.

Mom had a way of saying something to make you feel that you were not enough. For Paula and me, no matter how nice we looked, she would say, "You look good, but you have this one lock of hair out of place." She could never just say we looked good. I bring this up because even in death, she couldn't tell me that she was proud of me or anything nice without adding a negative to it. Her letter said something like she was happy I was doing well, but I had strayed from the path for a while before finding myself.

I read the letter, thinking she disapproved of the only positive normal time in my life that I had been straying from the right path. I think she was referring to my relationship with Kevin. I guess she didn't approve of us living together. I was more than heartbroken. She had shattered every positive thing I felt I had gotten from her. This coming from a woman who had ten children by at least three different men. She and Dad had also lived together before they got married. She and Dad got together in 1956 and were not married until 1967.

As I think about it now, years later, it still hurts and angers me. I threw the letter away. After the way she had lived her life, how could she judge me? She was so into the Bible; she knew the only one who can sit in judgment is God. I will have to answer to Him when I arrive in Heaven. My decisions are between he and me. She was not involved in my life except to overprotect me from my father and to judge my actions. She would make me feel guilty when I did come home because she would emphasize how far away I was.

Getting back to the time of the funeral, we had to wait until Friday for the service. We were told it may take up to a week to get Mom's ashes back. During the next few days, we tried to be patient and enjoy, as much as we could, the hot summer weather. We went to Henry's so we could all comfort each other. The creek was an inviting way to cool off while passing the time. Swimming and floating helped to ease our minds.

Paula was busy doing her normal visiting everybody routine. She and Tom stayed at Penny's (Harold's ex-wife), as always. She was selective about whom she visited. She claimed that Jordan was her hero, but she would never go to his house. It was the house Tom had grown up in. The house held bad memories for him, but Paula should have gone without Tom. It upset Jordan that she didn't bother to go there.

Paula came to Henry's when I was there. I felt so angry with her. I got up to leave when she arrived. She chased me out of the house, asking why I was so upset with her. I finally got the courage to tell her to her face. I was angry about the way she had treated me all those years. She always made me feel like I wasn't good enough for her. As a child, we had to share a bed. She would yell at me, "Stop breathing so loud!" She invited me to Elizabeth's wedding, but I had to stay in a hotel because she had family staying at her house. She had done this many times before— "can't stay at my house."

At Elizabeth's wedding, Paula basically ignored me. I cut her some slack because she was trying to make everything go as planned. The wedding was held at an upscale restaurant in St. Charles. Paula was making sure the food was being served, etc. It was very hot that day. I don't take the heat well, so Debbie and I sat in the shade as much as possible. Paula was going from table to table, talking to people as a good hostess should. I walked by her a couple of times, but she never introduced me to anyone.

When things started to settle down, I had an expectation that Paula would at least come to our table for a while. She did only to bring Brendon (her grandson) as she was showing him off to the guests. In one of my trips to the front for a drink, I overheard one of the guests say, "I think her sister is here." I answered yes, I was her sister. Debbie asked if we could leave. Back to the hotel? No, she wanted to go home. She felt the same as I did. We weren't wanted there.

Back to Henry's house. Paula was crying after I exploded on her. Mom had left a poem that she wanted to be read at the funeral. Paula was trying to ask me to read it. She said that Mom would have wanted us to deliver her message together. I gave in, but I was not happy. I did it for Mom.

The day of the funeral arrived. Mom's ashes had not arrived back to the funeral home. We proceeded without them. The interment of Mom's ashes would be at a later time, attended by the family who could be there.

The service went as planned, with Paula doing most of the talking. I read the poem Mom wanted. The church was about half full. Adam was not there since he had left to return to Florida the day after the planning session. We proceeded to the fire hall in Sidney Center for the after-service luncheon put on by the auxiliary service, which is customary in this area.

Debbie and Alisa were of great emotional support. I was not as upset with Mom's passing as I had been with Dad's. I knew Mom was in pain every day. She felt neglected by the family she had brought into this world.

The four of us returned to the hotel to get some sleep. We headed out the next morning for the long journey home. Four-hour drive to Philadelphia, then four-hour plane ride. We were mourning for Mom, but were excited to get back to the wedding plans and the wedding.

Since we had taken this detour from the wedding plans, James was asked to get a caterer for the food. He was supportive due to the circumstances. He arranged for a caterer but told them to deliver the food at 4 P.M. The wedding took place at 1:30.

The wedding day came. It was hot -97 degrees. We all arrived at the chapel. The bridesmaids and I were in the dressing room helping each other get spiffed up. Debbie looked so beautiful.

Alisa did as well. I was so happy. I could see in Debbie's face how much she loved Nick. I could see in Alisa's face how happy she was for Debbie.

Shane and Alisa drove out to the wedding together. While Alisa was getting dressed, Shane was outside with the groomsmen. He was smoking pot down near the cars. I think some of the groomsmen took part too. Shane wore sunglasses the rest of the day, inside and out.

The reception was at an apartment complex's indoor recreation center. The air conditioning could not keep up with the number of people. We had very hot, sweaty people waiting around for food. The food finally arrived a little ahead of schedule, which was good. Everyone started to relax after eating. Nick's Aunt Beth had made a three-tier cake. When she tried to put it together onsite, it fell apart. The place was too hot. The frosting was melting, and the cake layers were sliding off one another. I think we ended up eating the bottom layer only.

Nick was not old enough to drink legally, so I did not have to worry about alcohol. Most of their friends were not 21 either. We served punch at the reception with one exception. I had gotten enough champagne so that each person could have one glass to make the toast. I poured in the kitchen while my friends (Pat and Sherri) passed out the drinks. CJ's toast was heartfelt and warm.

The wedding presents were stacked on a table near the door. There was a basket for cards. Besides the wedding, I had arranged with a friend to send the kids to Austin for their honeymoon.

James gave the kids money to use on their honeymoon. Nick put the money in his jacket pocket. He hung the jacket on the back of a chair. Later, when the party was over, Nick got his jacket, but the money was gone. Someone from the wedding had stolen it.

Prior to the wedding, Alisa's run-ins with the law were mostly speeding tickets, drug possession, and burglary. After the wedding, she started getting violent. She was arrested in August and September 2011 for assault and battery. On the police blotter, she is shown as being a victim of burglary-forced entry on October 8th, 2011. It was a Saturday. I should have been home, but I do not know what this was.

As time went on, Alisa and I did not see too much of each other. I was out of town working while she was working and taking classes. When I was home, we would have coffee on the deck in the morning after she woke up. Working as a server until midnight or later, she never got up before 10. She would come upstairs, cigarette in hand (unlit, of course), pour herself some coffee, and go out onto the deck to soak up the morning sun. I would join her. It became a time I treasured. It never really lasted too long because she always had somewhere to be, but for that short time, it was just us. I miss those mornings.

The following year, 2012, seemed pretty uneventful in my mind. I think Alisa was on probation and was trying to keep from going back to jail. There are only two listings on the police blotter that year. On March 27th, she had a failure to appear. I think I was with her on that date. I remember going to the courthouse in Aurora. We were running late, and then we got held up in the security line. We got into the courtroom after the judge was done with the other cases. Alisa was marked as a no-show.

The other entry is from May 4th. The blotter shows she was a victim of a hit-and-run accident. The back bumper on the car was damaged. She took the bumper off. She went to a you-pull-it junkyard and got a replacement bumper. It was bright red while the car itself was maroon. Now the cops could really find her.

Debbie and Nick continued to have issues with Peggy. Both kids were working. Nick, for his Uncle Terry, delivering and setting up appliances purchased from Sears. Debbie was still working at Check into Cash. They had people living with them pretty much every day since the day they moved in. Nick's brother Tom stayed for a while. Ignacio (better known as Nacho) stayed as well. The people who came in and out of the swinging door at Nick and Debbie's were "friends." There were others, but I don't think any of them paid rent. These people did, however, cause large increases in the heating bill, cable bill, electric bill, and, of course, the food bill.

There were a number of times when Debbie would call and ask for financial help. I told her she needed to get money from her live-ins. She has a big heart like me, and can't turn someone out when they are down on their luck. It was very frustrating. I would give her money to pay the bills only because I could afford to. I wish I had the strength to say no.

I was letting Alisa live at home and paid the utility bills for her and me. I felt, to be fair, I had to help Debbie and Nick. I finally got so fed up that I invited Nick over and had a face-to-face, heart-to-heart talk with him. I explained that needing help when something went wrong, like needing tires on the car, was a completely different situation paying those utility bills month after month. I was going to turn off the Bank of Mom.

Nick didn't take my speech very well. It caused a rift between me, Debbie, and Nick. They started to distance themselves from me.

Alisa was on probation in 2012 and 2013. Her end date was September 30, 2013. Over the Labor Day weekend, I wanted to spend alone time with her. She hadn't violated her probation, so her probation officer allowed her to take a short trip with me. We took off for a four-day adventure into Northern New Mexico and Southwestern Colorado. Her probation officer had specified that she not leave the state, but one night in New Mexico did not seem like a big deal.

I was so excited to get her away during a time I thought she was sober. I'll never know if she really was, but I needed to believe it. We started by just going down Friday to Colorado Springs to go hiking at the Garden of the Gods Park, which is a favorite place for us. We had DJ with us. We went to the annual balloon festival and ate festival kind of foods. Walking around and talking was so enjoyable by this time in her life. She didn't remain calm too often. Her bipolar symptoms had become full-blown by then. At 26, she wasn't taking medication except to smoke pot.

We drove to Farmington, NM, and stayed the night. The hotel was not pet-friendly, but Alisa got DJ in and out without being seen. I give these kinds of details to give a better understanding of bipolar disorder. Rules don't apply to these people. For a parent, it is a constant battle, so you learn to pick your battles. Having a dog in a non-pet-friendly hotel was not a battle I felt needed attention. Besides, I liked Mutt Face. The following morning, we headed back to Colorado to the cliff dwellings.

The cliff dwellings are named Mesa Verde and are a known tourist destination, but not well-visited. We had a beautiful sunny day with very few other people around. We hiked and talked. The main attraction at the park is a complete dwelling preserved as it was found. You can go down into it by using a wooden ladder. Neither of us wanted to climb down. The ladder didn't look too sturdy to me. We were happy to stay up on the trail and look down. We wondered how the Indians had lived in such a vertical place. Little did I know that this would be our final adventure together.

When we returned from Mesa Verde, Alisa was done with probation. She started to party again. She still went to school and work. I went back to work as well. I saw very little of her again.

One Thursday, I got home late as usual. Alisa was at work. I went into the kitchen to find something to eat. Alisa had made brownies. I ate a couple of them and went to bed. I don't remember much of the next 36 hours. Here is what I do remember. I woke the following morning not feeling well. My balance was off, and the room was out of focus.

I must have made a loud noise because I woke Alisa up. She was quite concerned about my condition. She made me go back to bed. The next thing I remember is Audrey taking my blood pressure. (Audrey was a nurse by then.) It was late afternoon. She told Alisa to take me to the emergency room. I told Alisa to let me sleep. She did, but the following morning, she took me to the hospital.

Upon arrival, I was immediately taken to a room. Alisa was right there with me. The hospital took blood, which was run through the normal battery of tests. It came back that my glucose level was way above where it should be. I was diagnosed with having a mini-stroke. I was taken for an MRI of my head to look for damage.

As the day went on, I began feeling much better. My MRI came back normal. My glucose level was coming down, so the hospital released me with instructions to go to my doctor as soon as possible. Alisa took me home. She had to go to work. She helped me into bed before she left. I slept through the night.

The following morning, I got up feeling almost back to normal. When Alisa got up, we went out on the deck so she could smoke and drink her morning brew. We started talking about my experience over the last couple of days. It turns out, the brownies Alisa had made were marijuana brownies. I told her I had eaten a couple of them, and she was horrified. I may still have had a mini stroke, but I was higher than a kite. I was quite upset.

The brownie incident actually turned out to be a good thing. I went to the doctors as instructed. Due to the high glucose level, the "doctor's" diagnosed me as pre-diabetic. She warned me that I needed to start watching what I was eating or I would be insulin dependent. That was a wake-up call.

I was not going to be like my brother Ralph. He was insulin dependent but could not control his diabetes. He ended up losing some of his toes. At the end, he was on kidney dialysis three times a week. He died a slow and painful death. I took the doctor's advice and went to work. Alisa was my cheerleader now. She encouraged me every step of the way.

Using healthy eating habits and walking the treadmill every night, I lost fifty pounds. I went from a size 16 to a size 6. My A1C was 6.3. My doctor called me her poster child on how to do things right for your health. I was not ready to sit on the sidelines of my life and watch. To this day, I still try to eat right and exercise. I am a size 8 now with an A1C of 5.7, and I am okay with that. It has been ten years, and I'm still going strong.

I was so excited when Debbie told me she had finally gotten pregnant. The pregnancy was a long time coming. She had trouble conceiving, but the miracle finally happened, so I was going to be a grandma! Yeah! Alisa had said she would never have children, so it was up to Debbie. She was due in September.

I don't know Alisa's initial reaction because I didn't tell her. Debbie probably did. I know she was happy for Nick and Debbie. I believe she was jealous. She had said she never wanted to have children, which I thought was a good thing, unless she learned how to legally control her bipolar. Street drugs would not have been good for a baby.

I had to leave again to return to Boston. It was difficult to be away. At that point in time, I seriously considered ending my traveling, but the money was too good. The girls were learning to stand on their own feet, so I continued. Debbie and I were strained in our relationship due to my shutting off the Bank of Mom.

I was struggling with losing both my girls. Alisa to her drug life, and Debbie based on money. I wanted so much to be closer to both, but it was not meant to be. When I would come home on the weekends, Alisa would be working or just out. Debbie's schedule was too busy. She and

Nick helped his dad coach little league baseball. Every weekend, the kids would be at the games with no time for me. I can't even tell you if Debbie had morning sickness.

During the first part of Debbie's pregnancy, Alisa was coming and going as usual. She did become more agitated as time went on. We were arguing one day in the kitchen, and she blurted out that she was pregnant. Oh, no. A whole range of emotions welled up inside. I really did not want to believe her, but I was afraid not to. I just brushed it off.

From Easter until her death, Alisa was in Northern Colorado, being pretty much homeless. The next chapter details what I know of those last six months, so I'll end this chapter with the birth of my first grandchild.

Between April and October 2014, I tried to reconnect with Debbie. It was hard. Her mother-in-law and sister-in-law planned her baby shower. I think I should have felt left out, but between working and worrying about Alisa, I just let the Huttons handle it. I did attend the shower but felt totally out of place. Almost everyone there was either the Hutton family or Debbie's friends. I felt like the fifth wheel, so to speak. I continued to watch from afar.

Debbie's labor was induced on September 2, 2014. Nick had taken her to the hospital early morning. Labor progressed slowly. In the late afternoon, the doctor came to check on Debbie. She wasn't progressing as the doctor had expected. The doctor manually broke her water so labor would speed up. Nick stayed with Debbie all day and went back into the delivery room. Haley was born at 7:22 P.M.

Nick brought the baby out for the rest of us to see. He was such a proud papa. Haley was so perfect. Everyone from the waiting room gathered around. Debbie was moved to her room, and we all started to "get in line" to go in. I was so happy about being a grandmother. My mood was less joyful because I had Alisa on my mind.

I sent a message to Alisa telling her she was an aunt. She was happy for Nick and Debbie. She was also hurt because Debbie had said that she wouldn't be allowed in Haley's life. A couple of days later, I sent her another message with a picture of Haley. I was glad I had done that. I hoped that Haley's birth would bring the girls together, but it did not. Besides the picture, Alisa never got to see her niece. My heart still hurts for that situation.

# CHAPTER TWELVE

## *2014: The Road to the End*

In 2013, my brother Adam came to live with us after ending an abusive relationship in Florida. I suspected that Adam had a drug problem because of having visited him in Florida. He was on Xanax, morphine, and a couple of other things. While being unsuccessful trying to get Alisa help, now I had Adam to deal with. Alisa got moved to the back burner, so to speak. I spent a lot of time and effort when I was home to try to determine what disease(s) Adam really had. I asked for medical records. His primary care doctor in Florida had retired at the age of 75. Her records just showed Adam going in monthly to get a prescription for his morphine. The records from his hospital stated he had pancreatic cancer, which was completely untrue. He had never had cancer. However, he was convinced until his dying day that he had pancreatic cancer.

I got Adam a real primary care physician who referred him to a gastroenterologist and a cardiologist. After several visits and blood work, we had achieved some level of medical stability and proper treatment. I would fill his medication box for the week before I left and lock the rest up in my security box. Many times, he would call and say he was out of his pain medication. He would say that he lost them. He was always trying to get more.

I don't know what kind of relationship Adam and Alisa developed. I do know that with Alisa being gone so much, Adam became DJ's caretaker of sorts. DJ and Adam bonded quickly. DJ would keep Adam company by lying on his bed with him. Alisa was usually gone when I would come home, so our interaction was little at the time.

Adam knew Alisa had a drug problem. He would try to talk to her about it. She just blew him off. Her drugs of choice were ecstasy, cocaine, meth, alcohol and pot. One night, Adam called me, wherever I was, and told me Alisa was tripping. He said she had taken LSD and was having a bad trip. She had never touched the stuff, so it was hard to believe him. He said he would sit with her until she came down.

Colorado legalized marijuana for recreational use in 2013. Individuals can visit pot shops if over 21 and purchase marijuana like it is alcohol. Alisa had a medical marijuana license, so she could buy it long before the bill was passed. She also had many sources to obtain pot, which until 2013 were not legal. She would sell pot just as she did other drugs.

Once marijuana became legal, Alisa saw her pot market start to dwindle. Why buy from her and maybe get caught when people could just walk into cannabis shops and buy it legally? Her new marketing strategy was to buy cheap from her known dealers (or medical marijuana may have been cheaper than recreational) and sell for profit, but undercut the cannabis shops. I think this worked for a while.

In March of 2014, Alisa called me, crying, saying she had been attacked. I told her to call the police, but that suggestion made her hysterical. She just kept pleading with me to come and get her. She was in front of the 7-11 near the highway. I got in my car and drove to her location. She was lying on the ground, curled up in a ball. I asked for more details about what happened. She said three large Mexican dudes had beaten her up and stolen her weed. I was going to call an ambulance, but she threatened to run if I did. She wouldn't have gotten far, and seeing the condition she was in both physically and emotionally, I did as she asked and took her home.

The following morning, I convinced her to go to the emergency room. She did not want to go to the Aurora Medical Center, so I took her to the north side of town to North Suburban Medical Center. I didn't object because the hospital was closer to James, and I thought I might be able to get some support from him. He did come to see her. She was admitted to the hospital with an expected length of stay of about a week. She had suffered a skull fracture during the assault. Her head had been slammed against the sidewalk/curb.

I called James and told him the situation. He came by after work. I should have known better. Alisa was cooperative with the staff the first. James' visit went okay. The following day, Alisa was having cigarette withdrawal (and whatever else was in her system). She was becoming agitated and uncooperative. She kept asking the staff if she could just go outside and have a smoke. They told her no, that her head injury was too bad to get out of bed.

James came by again after work. What a disaster that was! When he came in, he was strutting like a peacock (typical gait for him). Alisa started with him. Did he have a cigarette? He told her that she couldn't smoke in the hospital. She started pleading with him. The more she pleaded, the angrier he got. They started a shouting match in the room. I tried to calm him down. I felt I had a better chance of him calming down than her. He did calm down for a short time, but then he was back at it. Staff came over to try to get them under control. I just stood there feeling defeated.

The doctor came in. Alisa asked if she could go have a cigarette. The doctor said, "If you walk out the door, you will be considered discharged against medical advice." She said she would come right back. I wanted the doctor to sedate her. I can't remember if either James or I asked, but it didn't happen. I think there was a medical reason for not doing it. James stormed out, saying she was my responsibility. She was 27. I was not responsible for her behavior. I finally left. Alisa was still trying to negotiate a temporary release.

The hospital released Alisa after only three days because of her behavior. They told me to make her stay in bed and be quiet. It was the equivalent of asking a dog not to chase a squirrel. I took her home and got her to lay down. She was exhausted from her ordeal at the hospital, so getting her down that night wasn't that hard. The next day, she was out the door as if nothing happened.

During the time between the hospital stay and Easter, Alisa was all over town and so out of control that little of what she did made sense to me. She would come home to eat and sleep. Then get up and, more often than not, start arguing with me. She normally took DJ in the car with her, but during that time, she left him home a lot. He was Adam's buddy. Many times, she would say that she was leaving to take someone to work who couldn't get there because their car had broken down.

I would give her money for gas sometimes. On one of those rescue operations, she ran out of gas. She called me to bring her money for gas. She was in North Denver in an area that I normally avoided. I was tempted not to go, but I was concerned about the repercussions if I didn't. The gas station was at least a twenty-minute drive from our house.

From the tone of her voice, I knew I had to make it a quick twenty minutes.

By the time I arrived, Alisa was fuming. She was sitting in her car. I walked up to the car and tried to give her a twenty, but she refused to take it. She started to scream at me. I tried to walk away and get in my car to leave, but she jumped from her car and started after me. She took my shoulder to turn me around, still screaming. People at the station were getting scared. That was the one time that I threw the initial punch but missed. She started trying to hit me, but I was able to block her until she got my face. She punched me right in the nose. Someone called the police.

Upon police arrival, Alisa took off in her car to who knows where. She did have the twenty dollars when she left. I was escorted into the gas station to be questioned. I told the police that she had attacked me, and I wanted her arrested. They went to look at the surveillance camera. When they returned, they said I could be charged because it looked like I was the aggressor since I had swung first. The situation was left as it was. No charges were filed against either of us.

Easter came along with Alisa's drama. I can't remember the actual trauma that happened that day. I know the following day, I went to the Arapahoe County Sheriff's office to file for a restraining order. I couldn't take any more, and I knew I could no longer do anything that would help her. The court approved the order. She was to be served by the sheriff. She was at work, so the sheriff waited in his car in front of the house for her to come home. As she rounded the corner, the sheriff stopped her by walking toward her. She stopped the car and was served. She yelled something at the house, then drove away.

We arranged a time when Alisa could come and get her stuff. She filled her car and came back in for DJ. Things got ugly really quick. Adam was holding DJ, and Alisa was trying to pull him away, but Adam held fast. Since Alisa had nowhere to go, Adam wanted DJ to stay with us. They were downstairs when the argument started, but moved upstairs as Alisa tried to pull DJ free. They went out on the deck and down to the lawn. Adam fell in a heap when she made her final pull. She took DJ to the car and roared away.

Alisa somehow ended up in Northern Colorado. She would go between Loveland and Fort Collins. She was couch-surfing for a while. It was summer, so she could sleep outside if need be. She met up with a group and started dating an older man named Matt. Her life got a little more stable for a while. Matt was with a group that was rehabbing some cabins in Loveland. The story I got was that these people could live in the cabins rent-free as long as they helped clean up the property and repair the cabins. The owner was trying to get the property ready for whatever he wanted to do next with it.

She and Matt shared a cabin. Matt would use her car (with or without permission, I don't know). She would call me occasionally from someone else's phone because hers had been stolen. Most of what she had had been stolen, except for clothes. She kept those in the trunk of her car.

On one occasion, Matt took Alisa camping. He had brought the tent but forgot the tent poles. Alisa climbed the tree, above where the tent was being set up, and tried to secure the tent to the lower tree branches. In doing so, she fell out of the tree and was stabbed in the side by something on the ground. Matt didn't think it was serious, and she had to beg him to take her for treatment. She ended up with stitches. I was not told at the time.

I found out about the fall when I went to James'. I don't know why I went there, but I did. I walked in to find Alisa lying on the couch. She told me what happened and that she was going to stay there for a couple of days. During that visit, she told me that she and Matt were engaged.

Alisa left James' house and went back to the cabin complex to find Matt had stolen things from her car. Matt was an alcoholic and having stolen things from her; she made the decision to leave. She went back to being homeless. She was back to roaming between Loveland and Ft Collins. She would still call me to say she was okay or if she needed something. I made a couple of trips to take her to Walmart to buy hygiene supplies and, of course, food.

During one call, Alisa said she was scared. She was manic, so she was talking very rapidly, and much of what she said I didn't understand. She talked about someone wanting to hurt her. I was out of town in the middle of Kansas, I believe, so I couldn't go to her. Instead, I used my Marriott rewards points and set up for her to stay in a hotel for a few days. She called me to thank me for the hotel room. She was thankful to get a hot shower and be able to sleep undisturbed. She was used to sleeping with one eye open. The call went to voicemail. That was the last voicemail I ever got from her. I kept it for a long time, but somehow, it got erased. I was very upset.

The last time I saw her alive was the end of September 2014. We had agreed to meet since her birthday was coming up. I took her to lunch and then to a thrift store, where she wanted a new purse, so I bought it. She needed new tennis shoes, so she found a pair of those too, which I also bought. I dropped her off at Walmart and gave her money so she could buy stuff that she needed, like shampoo, toothpaste, etc. She said everyone kept stealing hers.

The remainder of her life is unknown to me. I only know what she wrote to me in a couple of emails on October 6th, 2014. She was trying to clean up her act and get back to school. She said she already had her FASFA application completed. I had tried to reach her on her birthday, October 3rd, but was unsuccessful. I only know what the police had pieced together about her last hours.

I did not hear from her ever again. I continued to go to Boston. During that time, I was not returning to Colorado every weekend. Every other week, I would drive the four hours to New York and stay at Jordan's house and visit family. It had been a couple of weeks since I had heard from Alisa. As time went on, I really started to worry. I knew something was wrong. On the afternoon of October 9th, 2014, I was driving to NY on the Massachusetts Turnpike when an image of Alisa's face appeared before me. I could see her as clear as day. I got a heavy feeling in my heart because I knew something had happened.

I called James to see if he had heard from her. He hadn't. I waited for several weeks, hoping to hear from her. I went up to where she had been living in the cabins, and no one had seen her. I asked to see Matt, but he was nowhere around. While asking around, a guy on a bicycle said something about a body up in the canyon. Then he rode off before I could ask anything. I went driving around Loveland looking for her, just as I had driven around Westminster the night she jumped out of the car at Wendy's.

Finally, after weeks of waiting, I talked again to James, and he still had not heard from her. I said that we needed to file a missing person's report. During that conversation, I expected James to say that he would do it, but, like everything else, he did not say a word. I was in Boston working. When I got back to Colorado, I went to Larimer County and filed the report. The report was filed on November 15, 2014. The Larimer County Sheriff began to look for her.

I had to return to Boston, so the sheriff made sure they had my number. That week was so long. I was trying to work, but it was nearly impossible. I went into the boss' office and told him that I was sure something had happened to her. He used the now-famous expression "Do what you got to do."

I arrived back in Colorado on November 21. Adam had made a mess of the house again with his vomiting all the time. The walls in the bathroom were covered with vomit. I just cleaned it up like I always did. The next day, I left the house to run an errand. I hadn't gone too far from the house when Adam called to say the police were there. I turned around and went home.

I started up the stairs to the main level, where the sheriff and the coroner were sitting at the table. I asked if they had found her. The sheriff said yes, they found a body. Did Alisa have any identifying marks on her body? Did she wear any special jewelry like a necklace? I said that she had a tattoo on her back that was comprised of moons and stars. She had a lot of necklaces, but none that I felt she wore more than others. It was then the sheriff stated that she was deceased.

I cannot describe to anyone what it feels like to lose a child unless you have been there yourself. It is so debilitating. The loss may not seem to be physical, but the emotional, mental, and spiritual toll it takes on you causes physical pain. When I got the news, I went into shock.

I had always expected that Alisa would die before me. Once she got heavy into drugs, I felt I had lost the battle with her bipolar disorder. The news of her death was not a surprise, but it was very painful. I began to cry. Adam came out of the bedroom long enough for me to tell him that

Alisa was dead. He hugged me and then went back to his room crying. I called Paula. She and Tom were shopping in Popular Bluff. I told her that Alisa was dead. Paula started crying, saying, "Don't say that to me." She and Tom left the store, headed back to their house to pack, and left immediately to be at my side. They arrived early on Sunday.

The sheriff explained that the search had been going nowhere until they enlisted the help of Tyson, who had been with Alisa that night. He was in jail on unrelated charges. He was offered some kind of deal if he would show the police where Alisa could be found. Tyson directed the sheriff to Larimer County Route 74E, better known as Red Feather Lakes Road. Her body was under a tree between mile markers 9 and 10. She had been stripped naked, and her head was facing west. She could not be seen from the road. She had been there for approximately six weeks. The sheriff's department did a grid search of the area to retrieve any evidence that may have been left behind.

I told the sheriff I wanted to see her. She replied that I did not want to. I needed to remember her like she was in the photographs that covered my walls. The coroner began to explain the cause of death. The decomposition was so bad that the date and time of death were hard to determine. October 10th was the first date given. It was later pinpointed to be October 8th. The coroner agreed that I should not see the body. I asked for a copy of the autopsy report. He said he would send me a copy. He did not send one. I am grateful that he did not. To see in writing what she had suffered through would be something I could never unread and would have been more devastating than it already was.

The coroner explained to me that the skull fracture she had received in March had not healed. Alisa probably had headaches the remainder of her life. He indicated that the headaches would have continued to get more intense as time went on. He also stated with the number of drugs she had in her system, she probably was not aware of what was going on. He recommended cremation since her body was so badly decomposed from lying on the ground exposed to the elements for so long. The sheriff asked if I wanted to notify James or if I wanted them to do it. I let them do it.

I had to notify Debbie. I went to her home. She was devastated as well. She broke down crying and remarked about the last thing she had told Alisa. Debbie had told Alisa that she would never see her baby, and she did not want Alisa in her life any longer. Nick was with her, so I hugged her for a long time and then left.

I went to church. Since it was Saturday, there was a five o'clock service going on. I sat at the end of a row and waited for the service to end. I approached the pulpit and began talking with Pastor Dan.

He and Pastor Jim took me into a small room and prayed over me. I asked if the church would hold her funeral. With the answer being yes, I set up a time to come back and meet with Pastor Jim to put the service together.

I used the funeral home and crematorium in Loveland, where her body had been taken. Paula and I went there to arrange for her body to be moved from the coroner's office to their facility. They very gently explained the process and the cost. Many people purchase an urn for a loved one's ashes. I did not. Knowing that I would be burying her in NY once the ground thawed in the spring, I purchased a wooden box with mountains carved on it. Once the papers were signed and the box decided on, Paula and I returned to the house. We had been told that her ashes would be ready by Tuesday.

# CHAPTER THIRTEEN
## *Life Goes On*

After returning from the funeral home, I went to see James. He had been informed of the death by the sheriff as I was. I said, "We have a funeral to plan. Do you have anything that you want included in the service?" His reply: "I don't care what you do. She didn't like country music." Sue was standing there with her hands on her hips. She said, "Do what you want, and I'll pay for it. I don't know if I will ever see her again because I don't know if she believed in Jesus." The encounter left another scar on me. How could they be so callous?

I returned to the house, where Paula and Tom were looking for music and Bible verses for the service. After I had been home for a while, Adam came out of the bedroom as high as a kite. He had taken all the painkillers he had and was stumbling all over the living room. At one point he nearly fell down the stairs. He said that Alisa's death was his fault. The ambulance was called, and he was taken to the hospital. I remember crying and telling the paramedic to get him the hell out of my house. I couldn't deal with him at that time.

The following day, Paula, Tom and I met with Pastor Jim at Colorado Community Church. As we were discussing details, I told Pastor Jim that

I just couldn't understand why she was gone. He made a statement that I still think of today: "We have a merciful God. God saw that she was struggling in this world, and He decided she had suffered enough so He decided to take her home."

I spent the next couple of days writing Alisa's obituary and eulogy. I was trying to pour out her whole life in a short speech. I wanted people to know she was much more than her disease, which included her drug addiction. I wanted people to know what joy she had brought to my life. She had become my best friend. We often sat on the deck in the morning on weekends, drinking coffee and just talking.

I am very grateful to Debbie and the Hutton family for arranging the photo tribute to Alisa. I had been looking at so many pictures, and I wanted to include them all, but I knew that was impossible. Debbie took the pictures to Nick's Uncle Rick, who spent hours developing the musical tribute to Alisa.

I decided to have two funerals, knowing that the family in New York would not be able to come. Her Colorado funeral was on November 26th, 2014. This was the day before Thanksgiving that year. The church was about a third full. There was no visitation ahead of time. As people came in after signing the guestbook, I asked that they also fill out a memory card detailing one of their favorite memories of Alisa. Those memory cards make me smile to know that she was a much a star to the world as she was to me.

At her Colorado funeral, the biggest surprise came when Audrey arrived. When she had stopped at the house on Monday, she was nine months pregnant, ready to give birth any day. I told her that I would understand if she did not attend the funeral. She said, "Unless I am in actual labor at that time, I will be there." Audrey arrived, no longer pregnant. She had given birth during the night before. She told the hospital staff that she was leaving, and there she was. Alisa had been there for her, so she was going to be there for Alisa.

The service was about a half-hour long. I delivered the eulogy. Debbie stepped up to the podium to make her remarks. She had a very hard time getting the words out. Paula was up next. She made sure to state in her remarks that Alisa believed that Christ was her savior. By making this statement, she let Grandma Sue know that she would see Alisa again inside Heaven's Gate. Finally, James took his turn at the podium. He had no prepared statement, so he just said something like he loved her and would miss her. I really wasn't listening.

The photo tribute that Uncle Rick put together was beautiful. It consisted of three country songs and at least fifty pictures. I have a copy of the CD with the tribute. The church had made a copy of the service, which we took and played at the New York funeral. To end the service, we played *I Can Only Imagine* by MercyMe.

As the service ended, people began to come forward to say their condolences. I was confused. I guess I was supposed to go the back of church to form a receiving line. It is customary that people come to the house afterward as well. I did expect this. I had arranged for food to come from Uno Chicago Grill, where Alisa had worked. Having people there was uncomfortable for me. I do not make a good hostess.

In honor of Alisa, I had the emerald butterfly necklace she had purchased in Spain enhanced with a silver cross. The cross hangs on the butterfly's body. The symbolism of the necklace to me is Alisa's body has ascended to Heaven, where she has met Jesus' loving arms. I never take the necklace off so that she can be with me always. I can no longer hold her physically, but I can hold on to her spirit and love through this gift.

Debbie, Nick, Haley, and I arrived a couple of days prior to the New York funeral. I had carried Alisa's ashes to NY on the plane. Having a box on the plane like that requires proof of what is in the box. I carried a certified document from the funeral home with me.

Paula and I worked with the Unadilla Methodist Church to schedule the service. The service was to be on December 5th at 2 P.M. I knew many people got off work at 3 or 3:30, so scheduling at 2 made sense for those who had to take off work. They could work half a day and still attend. Paula made sure everything was going to be set up. The laptop with the music and the Colorado service on it. We needed two easel-like stands for Alisa's pictures and the big screen to play the video. There would be no burial since the ground was frozen. We would lay her to rest by interring her ashes in the spring.

Ann (Jordan's wife) and I went to look for a headstone. We headed to Franklin, where we knew there was a memorial place. Ann was driving, and as we neared this bend in the road, Ann said that she thought there was a place for headstones on that road. Ann turned right onto the road. We found the place and met the owner. He took me inside and we designed the stone. As we started back out to the truck, I noticed, along the garage in a corner, was a small headstone. It read: "Macie Colten, our little angel." I asked the owner about it. He said a woman and her mother had ordered it a few years ago but had never come back to get it.

I called Harold and asked who Macie was. (With such a big family and me living so far away, it is hard to keep track of them all.) Harold said that Macie was Jack's daughter. I told the owner and asked how much was owed on it. He said to never mind about the cost, just take it and see that Macie got her stone. Ann put the stone in the compartment on the side of the bed of the truck.

Neither Ann nor I told anyone about the stone. After the funeral, the Ladies Auxiliary had a meal for the family. Jack did not come because he was in the hospital. Near the end of the night, I gathered Jane (Jack's mom) and Mandy (his sister) together and asked Nick to bring the stone in from Ann's truck. I presented it to Jane and Mandy. They were both so touched that they began to cry. Paula remarked, "Even in her grief, she is still doing for others." I asked Jane where Macie was buried, and she said in the Sidney Cemetery next to her dad. She said she would make sure it got to its rightful place. I feel that this was an act from Heaven that Alisa was orchestrating.

Debbie, Nick, Haley, and I spent the weekend at Jordan's house. We were trying to relax and deal with our feelings. We got to spend time with Jordan and Ann, and Henry and Carol. None of them had met Haley yet, so it was a positive thing to bring up everyone's mood.

The good feeling did not last long. Jordan got a call on Monday, December 8th, from our sister-in-law Marie in Florida. Our brother Dan had died. Exactly two months after Alisa. Dan had a heart attack when he went to take a shower. When he didn't come out, Jonathan (his son) went to find him. He was already gone. We were all very upset, but Jordan more than the rest, I think. He kept saying that he was supposed to go first because he was the oldest.

Debbie and Nick had to return to Colorado for work, but I stayed in NY. I called my employer and told them we had another death in the family. I was not planning to go back to work that year. The employer was not happy. As the end of the year got closer, I was pressured to go back to work.

Marie was making funeral arrangements in Florida. The siblings were making plans on how to get there and where to stay. My Holiday Inn points came to the rescue as far as where to stay. I had enough points to get three rooms for two days without anyone having to pay anything. Jordan and Ralph in one, Paula and Tom in the next, Jennifer (Jordan's daughter) and I in the last. Not what I wanted because I am not fond of Jennifer, but I really didn't have a choice.

When the pastor arrived at the church for the service, he was about thirty minutes late. He had everything set up at the other church that he serviced; he was ill-prepared to deliver a eulogy. He delivered a generic eulogy and would refer to Dan by his legal name, Daniel. No one called him Daniel, except maybe Marie. No emotion in the service. When the mourners were asked if anyone wanted to say anything, Jonathan got up and spoke. No one else, not even Marie. I decided right then my brother was not leaving this world without some kind of personalization. I walked to the front of the church and talked about my relationship with Dan.

We were connected not only by blood but by the struggles we had with our children. I did not say this. I did relay a story about how Dan had bought me my first actual bicycle. Growing up poor, we didn't have much. I learned to ride a bike from a friend who would let me ride her bike occasionally. Dan bought a three-speed bike for me for my birthday.

When the service was over, Jonathan thanked me for standing up. There was to be a reception put on by the ladies of the church at another location. Marie had not had the money to pay for Dan's ashes. On the way to the reception, Jennifer decided it would be a good idea to take up a collection for Marie. She felt since we were family, we should all help out. Hello? I had just provided six nights in a Holiday Inn for us. What more did she expect? I had buried Alisa two months earlier, and no one from my side of the family helped me. Jennifer didn't even come to her funeral.

I returned to Colorado from Florida. I just wanted to stay at home in my house and grieve. That wasn't an option. I had bills to pay with very little money to live on. I pushed my loss far down inside me and just went on. Left foot, right foot, continue the march was all I could do. I finally went back to work in January 2015.

Until January, I was on autopilot. As Alisa's mother, I was responsible for settling her affairs. I contacted the school about her passing, but due to the news reports, they were already aware of it. I had to provide a death certificate to Social Security, the IRS, and her student loan provider. Her student loan was written off. She had unpaid medical bills from her hospitalization earlier in the year. Those had to be written off as well. I knew she used pawn shops a lot of the time. I made the rounds with a death certificate to all the pawn shops that I knew she had visited to check for any outstanding articles she may have pawned.

In May of 2015, the Community College of Aurora held graduation. At my request, the school granted Alisa her degree posthumously even though she was two classes short of finishing. The dean had asked me when I called in the fall if there was anything they could do for me. I asked them to recognize all the work that she had put in at the school. The ceremony was very emotional both for me and Debbie. After all other degrees had been given out, the chancellor announced that the school was honoring her with the very first posthumous degree given out by the college. All the people in attendance, the graduates, the parents, teachers, etc., gave a standing ovation for her. One of her classmates filmed it, and now I can watch it again whenever I need a pick-me-up.

June 26, 2015, I placed Alisa's ashes in the ground at sunset. Some of the family attended. I did not plan a formal graveside service, but had invited anyone who wanted to come. The headstone had been placed, and it was a warm sunny day. It was very hard to take what was left of her and place the box in the ground. Our plot is close to Mom and Dad, so I knew they would watch over her. I later got pushback from Debbie about why I had buried her in New York, where family couldn't visit her. The only family that couldn't visit was Debbie, James, and his parents. I really think it was James' words, not Debbie's.

In July of that year, we sold the condo that I had purchased as a rental property in January of 2011. Nick held me for ransom is how I looked at the situation. He was listed as the primary borrower. If I didn't split the proceeds with him, he wasn't going to sign the papers for the sale. I ended up giving in. We split the proceeds, with Nick and Debbie getting one quarter of the proceeds. I specifically told Debbie that the money was to be used for getting them caught up on the bills everyone had stuck them with. She said they would definitely pay off her car.

Debbie was usually my transport to and from the airport. A couple of weeks after getting the money from the sale of the condo, she came to pick me up in a new pickup truck. Not brand new, but a different vehicle than they had prior. Debbie was so excited. I was so angry. They had bought the truck for Nick. With Nick working for Uncle Terry, he decided he needed a better vehicle to help Terry. I told Debbie that I would not ride home in the truck. I would walk home.

We had a very heated discussion about the vehicle. It was cold, so she finally convinced me to get in. It was a silent ride home. I had given them all that money to help them get ahead, but they had to spend the money on what Nick wanted. I am still angry today because I could have had that money in my retirement account. I didn't think about it much until recently, when inflation started to go through the roof.

For the next two and a half years, I just existed. I was, as Pink Floyd says, "comfortably numb." In some ways, I still am. My life was on hold. I had to go through the motions of life while dealing with work, the trials, and being a first-time grandmother. My relationship with Debbie was strained, and being a traveling consultant, I missed a lot of time with Haley in her early years.

I went back to Boston to work, but my head and heart were no longer in the work. I slacked off. I had four team members. I would butt heads with Matt a lot. He was young and cocky. He was the young know-it-all. He and I were supposed to work together. He had a list of edits he was developing. I was supposed to duplicate those edits in what I was doing. He would never give them to me. He would send me a document with a link to open his database, but it never worked.

I wanted to quit my job in Boston. I felt that I could not quit due to all the upcoming court appearances I would be making. Boston was going to let me work from home the weeks I had to be in court. If I started a new contract, I would be in danger of losing it for requesting too much time off. I felt unsettled, angry, sad, and worthless. Arguing with Matt did not help my cause. It became a moot point when, in June, Boston let me go. I was hurt but relieved. I think this was the first time I was released from a contract before it ended. It would not be the last.

Being let go from Boston was a blessing in disguise. I was able to collect unemployment and be free to go to the trials when needed. However, I still could not grieve the way I needed to. I had to be strong to go to court to face the people who had killed Alisa.

In 2016, I got an assignment working remotely for a company in Des Moines. Being remote meant spending a lot of time in the house that we had shared as a family. I could no longer live there. With the help of Jeremy, I prepared the house for sale. I moved my belongings into storage. I went to live in Missouri again. Paula owned an assisted-living facility that has several individual apartments separate from the manor. She let me set up to live in one of the apartments until the house sold, and I could find a new one.

I would return to Colorado sometimes and stay with my friend Elaine. I got to see Debbie and Haley, but it was not like having my own house. I missed having Haley help me in the flower garden. She loved to dig in the dirt. I remember her with the shovel and pail digging while talking in her own language at the time. During these visits, Elaine and I would go house hunting. I had always wanted a mountain cabin, so that was my focus.

I am doing an injustice to Elaine's memory for not having introduced her yet. I met Elaine in 2004, after I started working at Kaiser Permanente. I had started learning Epic, and I was assigned to help support the billing department where Elaine worked. She became a very close friend. After Mom died, she became like a mother to me. She would give me advice or just listen to my ranting. She and her husband, Keith, occasionally helped Alisa out when I was on the road. She would give Alisa money for gas sometimes. Not often, but a couple of times. The biggest thing they did for her was to buy a battery for her car. She could not get the car started, so she called me. I called Elaine. Keith and she went to a car parts place and got a battery, which Keith installed. I paid Elaine back when I returned home.

Not having a home in Colorado, Elaine always let me stay at her house. Debbie would drop Haley off so I could spend time with her. Elaine cherished these visits as much as I did. Elaine got really sick with a third round of cancer. This time in her bones. I spent as much time with her as I could. We went together after Christmas one year to the Royal Gorge and took the train through the canyon. Both Keith and Elaine have died since, but they are always in my heart.

After the job in Des Moines, I had three more assignments before losing my job. I worked in Sacramento for a short while, then Upstate New York, close to where I had grown up, and finally Palm Springs. The Sacramento position lasted only three months due to poor job performance. The company wanted much more than I could give.

Upstate New York worked out fairly well. I moved into an apartment. I would see family in the evenings and on weekends. It helped to start to rebuild family ties. I could visit Alisa's grave when I wanted to and talk to her as if she was still with me physically. The job itself wasn't too demanding at first. As I gained trust with end users, I was looked to more often for answers than the staff. Finally, the pressure from the end users got to me, and I went on short-term disability.

I had applied for social security disability using a lawyer. I had applied on the post-traumatic stress disorder diagnosis. I could no longer focus and was physically affected by it. I had balance issues, so living in my mountain home became an issue. I expected instructions from the lawyer about what I could and could not do. She did not provide any guidance, and I had bills to pay. I was afraid of losing my house, so I took another assignment. I was denied Social Security because I was working. I fired the lawyer.

I started my final assignment in the spring of 2018 in Palm Springs, California. I was to backfill a position while the employee was off on disability. The organization kept me on even after the employee returned to work. This became a point of contention. The employee would ask me how to do something, then do what she wanted. When the system didn't work, the finger was then pointed at me. My boss was gone for a couple of weeks in October, so I went to the supervisor who was in charge and expressed my issues. When the boss returned, she determined that I was unhappy and I needed to be released from my contract early. I was surprised, but everything worked out for the better.

I reapplied for disability in January of 2019 and was approved. I started receiving benefits in April. Financial reality set in based on the amount that I would be receiving each month. The money was enough to cover the mortgage, but not much else. I had to sell my little slice of paradise. I could no longer afford to live in Colorado, so I went back to New York. The house went on the market in March and sold in June.

I received notice that Kimberly Guinn was up for parole. The hearing was to be in June. I couldn't believe it. She had been sentenced to twelve years. It had only been five. I was definitely going to be there. I prepared a statement to read at her parole hearing. It included knowing that she wanted to be with her children while I was suffering with the loss of mine. I also stated that I forgave her.

The parole hearing day came. I was escorted to a waiting room with two court workers. They were there to provide support for me. I said I had a statement to read. They said it is unusual for the court to allow a prepared statement to be read. I was required to read it to them before we went in. I did, and they approved what I was going to say.

I entered the room and there Kim was on the monitor with her parents by her side. I could feel the anger rising up in me. How could she be allowed to go free and see her children when I couldn't? Information presented showed that she had been cooperative with all the requirements to be granted parole. She had been taking classes on addiction. Her parents said she would live with them, but would not immediately be allowed to see her kids. That would come later. I read my statement. Kim cried when I said I forgave her. I ended with saying that I didn't feel she should get out. In the end, she was released and is still out today.

During this time, Debbie was not speaking to me again. I wasn't seeing Haley either. Debbie saw on the internet that I had my house listed for sale. She sent a text asking if I was moving. I just said yes. She did not ask where.

The end of June, I was back in New York. My belongings were in storage and I was living with my brother Charlie (better known as Tyke). The situation was difficult because Tyke had a degree of OCD and had lived alone for so long that we were bumping heads. I did my best not to upset him. I started searching for a house.

My house hunt was stressful because finding a house in New York is much different than finding one in other states. In other states, a person gets prequalified prior to going house hunting, so they know how much they can afford. Not here. I was prequalified and placed bids on several houses, but was outbid. I asked if I could be a backup bid, but the answer was no, so I went on to the next. Then I found out the house I really wanted was back on the market because financing fell through. It was too late to have that one since I just went under contract on the house I am in. I bought a HUD house, meaning it was a foreclosure that the FHA had taken back.

Closing on a house here also requires that lawyers be present. New York is the last state in the Union to continue to require legal representation when closing a real estate deal. There were many hurdles to jump through, including finding out at the last minute that there was an unpaid water bill of more than $1000. If I had closed with that bill out there, it would have been my responsibility to pay it. Closing was completed on October 7th, 2019.

I could not move in until a few days later. I had a local moving company move my things from storage to the house. The house had been empty for a couple of years, so there was no running water, no hot water, and no heat. No electricity was live either. It took until November or so to get the house in shape so I could stay here. Family helped me redo the kitchen and family room so I could stay here during the winter.

I have since completely remodeled the downstairs. My brother Jordan taught me a lot about construction and old houses. Jordan built a deck on the back after removing the rotting porch. I am now working on the upstairs. The house is finally starting to feel like home.

By working on the house and writing this book, I have finally been able to grieve and let go of the hurt. Rebuilding this house has symbolized rebuilding my life. Each screw, each nail and every piece of drywall I installed was a symbol of hope for tomorrow. Each section of lath, plaster, and blown-in insulation that I tore out was another bitter memory being laid to rest.

I am disabled due to post-traumatic stress and major depression. I try to find joy in each day. I live alone except for my "kids," Lady and Sassy, two German Shepherd rescues who have helped to rescue me. I sit on the deck with my coffee in the quiet of the dawn and watch my dogs play. I hope Alisa is watching with me. I miss our coffee time.

# CHAPTER FOURTEEN

## *Trials*

There were five people involved in Alisa's death. There were three men and two women. They were captured fairly quickly. I think the first two were arrested within days of her discovery. I think those two were caught on the day of Alisa's funeral, November 26, 2014. The other three weren't on the loose much longer. I think they were all in jail by Christmas.

There was going to be five separate trials because the attack and murder was a conspiracy. This meant months of hearings, motions, and trials. I was not prepared for what was going to happen over the next two-plus years. Initially, I was hoping for the death penalty for the two oldest men who had coordinated the whole plot. I wanted revenge. I wanted them to suffer the way they had made Alisa suffer. I wanted to build a cage and put each one separately into the cage with my brothers.

The detectives and district attorney worked diligently to interview each defendant and try to get one to flip on the others. Tyson (who had been with Alisa that night) was not arrested, and I wondered what his role in the plot was. He led detectives to her body. During the interviews, it was uncovered that he was a victim of the assault as well. He did not get the extensive treatment that was given to Alisa, but he was beaten and coerced into going along with the plan. He did not hurt her, but he was made to convince her to come out of the apartment and get into the waiting car outside.

April 1st, 2015, was the second worst day of my life. During this first court hearing, all the details of the case were laid out. Every step of the kidnapping, beating, torture, rape, and murder was presented. The hearing lasted eight hours. Those eight hours seemed like an eternity. Every detail was another stab in my already broken heart. Paula and Tom had come out from Missouri. Debbie, Nick, and James were there. The was a lot of crying by Paula, Debbie, and me. There was a lot of anger and rage in Nick. I couldn't look at James because I felt he had failed to protect her, just as I had. I cried all day. There were times that I couldn't catch my breath. There were crime scene photos that were used, but those photos were turned so we could not see them. However, there was one that I got a glimpse of. It was her jawbone.

The timeline of events is clear to me, but the timeframe is not. I understand that she died on October 8th, but these events took place over a period of a couple of days. Her last hours were spent lying naked on the cold Colorado ground in a drugged and beaten state. She laid there long enough for hypothermia to set in and end her life.

This is the account of what happened to the best of my recollection. Let's start by saying upfront that Michael Bensen (boss man) was a drug dealer. Alisa was homeless. However, she was always picky about her personal hygiene. She had stolen shampoo, toothpaste, and some other hygiene products from Michael Bensen sometime earlier. This was first stated as the motive. Bensen wanted to make an example of Alisa. He wanted everyone to know that you don't steal from him. During questioning later, Bensen revealed that the attack was prompted by Alisa's cooperation with law enforcement over a prior drug case.

The incident started at Patrick Hannon's apartment in Fort Collins. Tyson and Alisa went to Hannon's apartment to buy drugs on October 7th. Hannon stated that the drugs were not there; they were in Loveland. Michael Bensen, Patrick Hannon, and Jose Rosario took Tyson to Loveland to get the drugs. (I am unsure if they actually got any drugs.) On the ride to and from Loveland, Hannon and Rosario were attacking Tyson, beating him with a collapsible baton. At one point, Bensen stopped the car, and all three men were beating Tyson. They were careful not to bruise Tyson's face. They wanted to use Tyson to get Alisa out of the apartment. They beat him to make him comply. They said if he said anything to alert Alisa of what was explained to him as a kidnapping, he would face further, more intense violence, which Tyson understood to maybe being killed.

While the men were gone, Alisa needed to go get cigarettes, so Kim Guinn went with her. That was Kim's assigned role in this plot. Make sure Alisa never gets away. The two went to a 7-11 with DJ. Alisa and DJ are seen on the store's video camera sometime around 2 A.M. Cigarettes were purchased, and the girls went back to the apartment. Alisa fell asleep.

This was the first place she probably felt "safe" enough to be able to sleep. She had been drinking and smoking pot. There were other drugs in her system that night as well: methamphetamine and cocaine.

On the return from Loveland, the three men stopped to pick up Chataigner McCaffrey-Pickett. Kim Guinn and Alisa were at the apartment. Alisa was still asleep. Tyson woke Alisa and coaxed her into going outside. DJ was right behind. There were two cars sitting at the bottom of the stairs going down from the apartment. Alisa and Tyson were forced into one of the cars. DJ jumped in with Alisa. She was in the back seat with McCaffrey-Pickett on one side and Guinn trying to get in on the other side. Alisa suddenly realized what was happening and started fighting back. She tried to get out of the car. She kicked DJ to get him out, but neither were able to get out. McCaffrey and Guinn started beating Alisa. Alisa was kicking, screaming, and biting, but to no avail.

Tyson was forced into the front seat, and the car took off. It was driven to Larimer County Road 54G to a residence of someone that was known by the group. The owner was at work, but his wife was there. She was under the influence of something. One of the group members told the wife that they were going to use the barn. She said they could, but they had to be gone before her husband got home from work. She didn't seem to realize the situation was serious.

The barn was a short distance away, but far enough so that noise coming from there could not be heard in the house. In the barn was an old mattress on the floor. Bensen and Hannon pulled Alisa from the car and threw her on the mattress, where they took turns raping her. They used her sweatpants to tie her hands.

Rosario went up to the house to get a gun. The beating had started when Rosario returned carrying the gun. Bensen pummeled Alisa with a duct-taped roll of quarters in his hand. It was equivalent of using brass knuckles. The other members of the group choked and beat her with the collapsible baton used on Tyson earlier. McCaffrey was using a stun gun on her. Bensen hit her with such force in the face that everyone could hear her jaw shatter. McCaffrey stomped on her head so hard that there was a squishing noise, indicating her brain had just been damaged. Rosario was strutting around, waving the gun when he was not participating. Reports indicated that Guinn did beat Alisa but remained somewhat away from the group. In all, the five attackers continued to torture her until she was unconscious. The deputy district attorney stated it was a night of astonishing physical violence.

Alisa laid on the mattress moaning when Hannon and Bensen picked her up and threw her in the back seat of one of the cars. Tyson was forced into the back seat on the opposite side of the floor. Bensen started the car and left. Alisa eventually ended up on the floor as well. Bensen drove to a remote section of Red Feather Lakes Road. On the side of the road between mile markers 9 and 10, he pulled Alisa from the car. She was semiconscious. Bensen tried to slit her throat, but she was flailing around so he ended up just stabbing her in the neck. He then left, leaving her on the side of the road. She was still alive.

Bensen drove Tyson back to the apartment, where he was allowed to shower. He was then released with the understanding to keep his mouth shut. In the morning, Bensen drove back to where he had left Alisa and rolled her down the embankment, where she ended up underneath a tree. He proceeded to finish removing her clothes so she would decompose faster. He also positioned her body with her head facing west. It could not be determined if she was alive when Bensen revisited her. The coroner's official cause of death was threefold: blunt force trauma to the head, stab wound to the neck, and hypothermia. The coroner stated that she had lain there for hours.

The first defendant to be tried was the leader, Michael Bensen. The above account of what happened was laid out. After all the details were laid out, court was adjourned for the day. At this point, we were under the understanding that a trial would be held for all defendants. Each one would be separate, so the length of time to the end of it all could be years.

If you are not aware of trial procedures, delays are common. Motions can be filed by either the district attorney or the defense. Motions were filed during the summer. In addition, there can be a continuance. This is usually done when some part of either side is not ready. Waiting on a result of a DNA test can cause a continuance.

During the summer, the district attorney worked with all the defendants to make plea deals. I was angry about them being able to plead out. The district attorney felt it was best way to go. If each accepted the plea deal, it would mean that there would not be any long, drawn-out trials. And if they testified against Bensen, their actions would be considered by the court.

The first part of the deal was that the death penalty would be removed from the table. I was really upset about that turn of events. The district attorney convinced me it was the right thing to do in order to get as much information as possible from the other defendants. It would help ensure that Bensen was convicted.

Now that each had taken a plea, meaning they admitted they did certain things, it needs to be clarified that no actual trials with testimony and a jury were going to take place. Each proceeding was going to involve the prosecution's case, then the defense trying to mitigate the extent of involvement. The defendant would be allowed to speak. I was the last to speak. Once all the above was completed, the judge handed down the sentence.

Each proceeding was going to be in the same format, so I will outline it for this first case, but only give changes to the remaining four. The hearing started with the district attorney stating the facts that were found by the sheriff's deputies. Next, it was the defense's turn. They tried to poke holes in the story told by the prosecution. Once each had made their case, the judge would consider what was presented and make a ruling.

Michael Bensen was charged with first-degree murder, kidnapping, conspiracy, and sexual assault. He was escorted into court on December 16, 2015, wearing the standard, orange-colored jumpsuit. He was handcuffed and shackled. His mother was in the gallery. He glanced in my direction, making my blood boil. This slimeball had killed my daughter. I wanted to shout and scream at him. Nick wanted to jump the rail between the gallery section and where the defense table was and beat the shit out of him.

The district attorney started describing in detail the role that Bensen had played in Alisa's murder. During that time, Bensen started taking notes. He kept turning his head to look in our direction with a smirk on his face. I just stared back at him. I was not going to allow him to intimidate me. He was thinking he was a badass who could get away with anything.

The major things brought up by the district attorney were how Bensen planned the whole thing. How he had been in charge of the kidnapping. He sexually assaulted her. Next, he used a police-like baton and a fist pack of quarters to beat her. He broke her jaw. Finally, after beating her, he drove her up to the mountains, dragged her out of the car and tried to slit her throat. He pushed her over the edge of the embankment so she could not be seen from the road. The following morning, he returned to the site. He removed what clothes she still had on and laid her head so she was facing west. He wanted her body to decay faster.

The role of Tyson was brought forth. In doing so, Tyson was described as a victim. Tyson had some mental health issues that were not stated by the prosecution. He had been a drug addict as well. The district attorney explained that Tyson feared for his life. He had been beaten and coerced into participating. He did what he was told.

Next up was the defense. I only half listened to what they were saying. Any argument trying to convince me that Bensen was innocent was beyond my comprehension. To try to show remorse, Bensen would occasionally grab a tissue and dab his eyes and nose. His mother was in the gallery and audibly sobbed. I started to listen more closely when they tried to discredit Tyson as a credible witness. With his relapses in memory, his drug abuse, and his overall state of mental health, the defense stated that he could not be believed. The defense also pointed out that Tyson had not gone to the police immediately after being released by the gang. He waited six weeks before coming forward. He also continued to hang around with Bensen and his gang.

Once the defense was finished, Bensen was allowed to make a statement. He referred to his notes before standing. He was quoted as saying, "I didn't do most of what they're saying. But I did do plenty." He added that he hoped our family could find peace.

I was allowed to speak before the judge sentenced him. I had two pages of notes where I outlined how much I missed Alisa. I was a total mess. She did not deserve what she got. I also stated that evil exists in the world, and Bensen was quite an example of it.

The judge started to talk. In a scornful manner, he was critical of Bensen for his drug-induced involvement with the most horrifying case in Larimer County in recent memory. He used the words "torture," "inhuman," and "unconscionable." "They are all accurate. It is horrific." He then handed down the sentence of 75 years in prison. This is the maximum sentence allowed for murder, kidnapping, and criminal trespass charges. Bensen is serving his time in a maximum-security prison in Colorado.

Patrick Hannon was charged with first-degree murder, conspiracy to commit murder, sexual assault, and kidnapping. He was the next defendant to be tried. He was brought to court on February 18, 2016. The prosecution began by saying Hannon's involvement was not as significant as that of Michael Bensen. They stated that his actions were "egregious." His actions included sexually assaulting and potentially raping Alisa in the back of his car, choking her in the barn until she turned blue and cleaning his car of incriminating evidence instead of calling for help while Alisa lay in a remote area dead or dying.

Hannon did conspire with the others to move Alisa's body from the barn. Hannon stayed at the barn while Bensen took Alisa up to the mountains "to finish her off." During the time Bensen was gone, Hannon was cleaning his car of any evidence that could be used against him.

"He knew what he did, and he knew he was involved, but instead of helping, he immediately went into self-preservation mode," the district attorney said. "He had every opportunity to do the right thing … but he never did." The actions Hannon took were pieced together from testimonies from the other attackers. He had told the district attorney he was high on methamphetamine during the attack.

The defense tried to cast doubts on the stories told by the others involved. They argued that Hannon wasn't "calling the shots" on that fateful night. The others were "throwing him under the bus" for their own benefit. The defense pointed out that the others had extensive criminal histories.

When Hannon was allowed to talk, he showed signs of remorse and bore a somber expression when he addressed the court. His brief statement was "I'm sorry to Alisa's family for what happened to her. I know it may not mean very much at this time, but I am very sorry."

Again, I was allowed to make a statement. I made the same statement I had made previously. I would give the same statement at each proceeding. Each defendant would know what they had done to me and my family.

The judge was unyielding in his sentencing and put little stock in the defense's arguments that Hannon's involvement had been exaggerated. He added that a maximum sentence was appropriate for the nature of the crimes and would benefit the community's safety. "If you can do it once, whether it's drug-induced or drug-related or none of the above, it certainly could happen again," he said.

Hannon was given a sentence of sixty years total. Forty-eight for second-degree murder and twelve years for first-degree kidnapping.

Kimberly Guinn was the next defendant to be brought to court. She had been charged with first-degree murder, conspiracy to commit murder in the first degree, first-degree kidnapping, and second-degree kidnapping. Guinn had plead guilty to one count of conspiracy to commit second-degree kidnapping in August of 2015. She appeared in court on Thursday, March 10, 2016. She had nearly twenty family members and friends in attendance.

I was the first one to speak at Guinn's proceedings. I spoke just as I had in the first two cases. I talked about Alisa's life full of love, travel, and friends. I acknowledged that Alisa had an issue with drugs that stemmed from a lifetime of struggle with bipolar disorder. As Alisa got older, she tried to self-medicate. It took years for her to admit she had a problem. She did not want the stigma that went with it. Alisa was committed to her education and wanted to become a counselor to help those with the same problems that had plagued her life. She was two classes away from her degree at the Community College of Aurora.

Continuing on, I stated how much I miss her. "There is a deep sadness in my soul that will never go away. My daughter had mental health issues, but she had a heart of gold. She did not deserve what was done to her." I told the judge that Guinn deserved more than the maximum sentence allowed and hoped that he would sentence her to the twelve-year maximum.

When I had finished speaking, the investigator spoke to the court about the day she had to inform me that they had found my daughter's decaying body on the side of Red Feather Lakes Road about 9.5 miles west of U.S. 287 in November 2014.

"While sitting at her kitchen table, I saw family pictures on her wall," Servin said. "Alisa smiling at the beach with her mother and sister, pictures of Alisa as a young girl. I knew in my heart the information I was about to give her would destroy her life." Having a daughter just two days younger than Alisa, the investigator said, made this case hit close to home.

The district attorney spoke next. Guinn's involvement started with keeping Alisa from leaving the apartment. Alisa was allowed to go to the convenience store, but only with Guinn following along. When put into the car for the ride to the barn, Guinn forced Alisa in and began punching her. Guinn participated in what was described previously as a "night of astonishing physical violence." Her testimonies were slightly inconsistent over time. He indicated that Guinn was hesitant to take a plea deal and serve as a witness until one of her codefendants accepted a plea deal. The district attorney made sure to recognize that Guinn had been the least directly involved of the five defendants in the case. He asked that Guinn be given the maximum sentence of twelve years for first-degree kidnapping.

Guinn's defense attorney started his portion of the hearing with several of Guinn's family members being allowed to address the court. This included her father and stepmother, Scott and Debbie Guinn; her mother, Kellie Guinn; her daughter, Karissa Guinn; and her sister Kristie Guinn.

They all spoke of Guinn's drug addiction and lifetime of physical abuse that had caused Guinn to lead a troubled, drug-filled life. They outlined much of the same kind of life Alisa had lived—poorly treated mental illness resulting in a drug-filled life.

"For the family we have prayed for you, we have prayed for Alisa," Scott Guinn said. "We ask God to give everyone strength to get through this. We want as much as possible to comfort all of you, but know it is not possible."

The defendant's daughter told the court that she knew what it was like to grow up without a mother, and she did not want her two younger siblings to know the same way of life. "I love her with all my heart, and I still need her," Karissa Guinn said. "And I still want her here with me. She has so many people who love and care about her and will never give up on her. She is not a lost cause."

The defense attorney argued that, unlike her codefendants, Guinn did not assault Alisa before she was killed. "One thing she always maintained is that she never hurt Ms. Smith," he said. "… The truth is, Kim did not assault Alisa; in fact, she tried to protect her from (McCaffrey-Pickett). It's just the facts, Your Honor. It was her nonviolent character showing through the haze of drugs and chaos." He asked the judge to sentence her to four years in the Department of Corrections.

The judge determined that Guinn should be sentenced to the full twelve years. "She is culpable of really a lot more than this amended account reflects," he said. "Because of that, the Court agrees with (the prosecution…..) It would depreciate the seriousness of what happened to give her anything less than the maximum sentence, I agree. A twelve-year prison sentence is appropriate."

Chataigner D. McCaffrey-Pickett was defendant number four. She appeared in court on April 7, 2016, along with Jose Rosario. I will give the events of McCaffrey-Pickett first. She was charged with first-degree murder, second-degree kidnapping, and conspiracy to commit murder. She agreed to plead guilty to first-degree assault with a deadly weapon.

The district attorney began outlining the details of McCaffreyPickett's involvement in the death of my daughter. She had sat on one side of Alisa in the car on the way to the barn. During that time, she was punching Alisa anywhere she could. Once the group arrived at the barn, McCaffrey landed the first punch that crumpled Alisa to the concrete floor. She used a taser on her, but the most horrific thing she did was to stomp on Alisa's head so hard that everyone could hear Alisa's brain squish.

The district attorney told the court that McCaffrey changed her story several times during the investigation. When she stomped on Alisa's head, it was the beginning of the end for Alisa. The violence erupted after that, so McCaffrey's foot played a major role in getting things started. He also stated that the sentence in this case should be the 32 years available. She received a better deal than she could have expected if she was brought to trial.

"Ms. McCaffrey came forward," the defense attorney argued. "She came forward early; she was the first one to come forward. She all along has said, 'I want to tell them what happened, I do not want to go to trial....' I think that is important. The idea is to give the court a complete picture."

It was made clear that she was the first of five suspects to accept a plea deal and agree to testify against her four codefendants. That cooperation, her defense attorney argued, was not adequately represented in the presentencing report, which is a compilation of information used to recommend an appropriate sentence to the Court.

McCaffrey had experienced a troubled childhood with a mother who was addicted to drugs, including methamphetamine, according to her defense attorney. McCaffrey wiped her eyes and sniffled during the proceedings.

I was allowed to speak before the judge handed down the sentence of the recommended 32 years in prison. She was given credit for time served of 496 days.

Last but certainly not least, Jose Rosario was brought forward for his sentencing. He was originally charged with two counts of second-degree murder, conspiracy to commit murder first-degree, and first- and second-degree kidnapping. He pleaded guilty to second-degree murder.

The district attorney stated the State's case against Rosario. Rosario did not physically assault Alisa but incited the violence when he told the group to "shut that bitch up." He has an aggravated criminal history. His history is the longest of the five defendants'. "The defendant, as he sits here today, has received a massive benefit compared to the risk he would face at trial," the district attorney said. "He's facing a second-degree murder conviction and a possible forty-year sentence versus what would have been a mandatory life-in-prison sentence if convicted at trial. I believe it is a windfall he never had to follow through."

The defense argued that Rosario grew up in an abusive household with no positive male role model to guide him. "While his world view and perspective doesn't justify or excuse his actions and decisions, those decisions are a bit more understandable," Collins said. "When one considers his mindset to ignore, avoid, and escape from potential trouble."

The defense hoped that this sentencing would bring peace to me and all of my family. This was the last sentencing. It has not brought peace. The pain has eased some, but more healing needs to happen.

Rosario addressed the court by stating, "Hindsight is 20/20— yet there is no beauty in it for me," Rosario said. "More like a lake of destruction, loss, pain, and addiction of all sorts. The drugs and the lifestyle consumed me. I became someone I no longer knew. There's not a day that goes by when I don't replay all the 'what-ifs'. It haunts me, as it should."

I spoke next with the statement I had made at prior sentencings.

While considering the sentence, the judge took in the fact that Rosario was the most remorseful of any of the defendants. He also considered the "assaultive behavior" demonstrated by Rosario, which included a lengthy served sentence for sexual assault. The judge handed down the maximum sentence of forty years in prison.

# CHAPTER FIFTEEN
## *After-Life Messages*

I have already mentioned the vision I had of Alisa in October 2014, which made me think she was dead. I was convinced that she would not be found alive.

I was driving from Boston to Upstate NY for the weekend in early November. I was on Interstate 88 near Cobleskill. I had K-LOVE on the radio, and they began to play "I Can Only Imagine." As the song began to play, I had a very vivid vision of Alisa standing next to Jesus with her elbow on His shoulder. She looked at me with a smile on her face and a twinkle in her eye. She said, "Hi, Mom. I want you to meet my new friend. His name is Jesus, and He loves me." I pulled over to the side of the road and cried for a long time. She was telling me that she had made it home and was safe.

During the summer of 2014, I tried to start a thrift store in Otego. I was selling used clothes, furniture, videogames, toys, and whatever I could find. The store was decorated for Christmas when I learned of Alisa's passing. I was sitting in the store one afternoon, all by myself, trying to decide what I was going to do with the store, when suddenly some of the toys started making noises. There was a music box that started to play along with some educational toys that talked to you. I know I had turned them all off because I was closing the shop for the day. I knew Alisa was with me.

When Debbie, Nick, Haley, and I arrived in NY for Alisa's second funeral for the family, we were invited to stay at Jordan and Ann's house. Debbie, Nick, and Haley took the bedroom that I normally slept in when I would come over from Boston. I went up to the bedroom to talk to Debbie and Nick. Haley was lying on the bed next to Nick, looking straight up at the ceiling, smiling and giggling. Debbie had tried to get her attention, but Haley would not stop looking at the ceiling. We felt that she could see her Aunt Alisa.

I had gone back to work in January in Boston. It was difficult. Anyway, I was having breakfast in the hotel one morning. The radio was always on during breakfast. The radio started to play "Survivor" by Destiny's Child. This song was one that Alisa often sang. I listened with sadness.

Saturday, June 13, 2015, I was home for the weekend by myself. The playpen was set up for Haley. Suddenly, one of the toys in the playpen started going off. I can't remember which toy, but I had many toys that played tunes. Again, I felt Alisa's presence.

I could not physically bury Alisa until spring. The cemetery administrator called to say the ground had thawed enough for the burial. I gathered family members who wanted to come. On June 26, 2015, I said my final goodbye to my baby. I placed her ashes in the ground at sunset. As I did so, I felt a warmth come over me. I looked up to the old pioneer cemetery across the road and could almost see Alisa in the sky above.

Alisa has come to me in dreams at times. Not that I remember them now. I just get the warm feeling that she is loved and happy. After I bought my new house up on Pike's Peak (9,000 feet up the mountain), Paula had a dream where Alisa came to her. She told Paula that she was glad I moved up there because I was closer to her. At that elevation, we were sometimes above the clouds. Therefore, Woodland Park is known as the city above the clouds. Some days, in the early morning, the clouds hang in the valley that is Woodland Park. I was above the city, so I could look out and see a beautiful layer of clouds, and I feel that I was looking at what I thought Heaven may be someday. I can almost see Alisa walking toward me with her arms outstretched, inviting me to join her. Sunbeams radiate from her face. I know that someday I will be with her, but until God decides on the time of the reunion, I will continue to pray for strength and healing.

This book has been healing for me. I hope that it helps to comfort someone who reads it. Know that you are not alone. Don't give up. Keep fighting the good fight for you and that person you love. Take one day at a time and enjoy the good things. Life changes in a flash, and you can't relive the moment.

# CHAPTER SIXTEEN

## *In Her Own Words*

## *Turning Point (2003) Journal Entries*

### Introduction

These entries came from a journal Alisa kept while she was in Turning Point in Fort Collins after her first arrest for intent to distribute cocaine. Some of the wording may be offensive but I feel in order to understand her mind, her thoughts must be read. She went to Turning Point in March of 2003 but these are the only journal entries that exist.

**June 17, 2003**

I am in scrubs and on house-freeze and outta of treatment!! For a week! They haven't approved my dad. I don't get my pass this weekend. My mom even talked to Kim Jones and not shit got done!! How ghetto, right?? I don't even get my full pass back till July 5, 2003! We aren't allowed passes on July 4th.

52 days till court!!

I've only had family therapy 3 times since I've been here. 3 months I've been here! Seems like fuckin' eternity!! 86 days I've been here. Since

March 23! God damn I've been here way too damn long! I need a cigarette. I need a break.

I'll be back!!

Anyways this blows hardcore. I need some serious help!!

Courtney straight jacked my CD!! Damn her!! If she doesn't give it back, I'll be really pissed off. Like REALLY pissed off.

Well, gotta do something production so peace!

## Things to tell Mom

* I had $4 from allowance, $2 spent on lunch and $1 lost to pay phone trying to call without costing anything. I have $1 for lunch on Thursday.
* sent you and dad emails
* Kim Bappe
* one week OT/HF (out of therapy/house freeze) 3 days in scrubs
* I hate my life!!
* Couldn't get a hold of Peter/Shawna
* Get me in another placement
* Good on test
* didn't approve dad still (Shawna could've done it @ staffing
* WANT TO GO HOME!!
* God damn it. I hate this world.
* What are we gonna do about the 72-hour pass for vacation? Talk to Shawna about it first.
* What if they make me get a new sponsor?
* Stress of school and SIR! * Restitution /letter from Broomfield
* Pass this weekend?
* I want to be like Kim!!

* I want to leave TP/Aug. 1 when school ends
* What NA and AA meetings are on the weekend? I'll please Chris and sit in on a few! Just so I can get my passes, HELL Yeah!

Anyways gotta go

Always

Alisa

**June 18, 2003**

UUH!! I feel like shit! I'm still in scrubs tomorrow and transition is pissing me off! They are listening to my CDs right now and can watch TV and do what the fuck they want. Their level 1's get till 10:00 pm. Level 2's 10:15 pm and level 3's 10:30 pm. Phase 2's in residential have only till 10:00 pm. They only have to do 3 groups a week and 4 meetings, and they get to choose which ones.

I HATE MY LIFE! ALL OF A SUDDEN THINGS SUCK SO BAD!

It's not right that transition is this much different, and we aren't even allowed in there! Screw that!! I want my CD's, yeah mine. I feel so screwed. I need to sleep. This isn't helping.

Always

Alisa

Resentment transition -Phase 2 get more "standard" privilege.

Phase probation should still restrict TV and radio for transition.

**June 19, 03**

Wow, once again something weird on the bus. Laura Donn, the one from Hobby Lobby. I didn't say anything to her, but it's still cool to see her again.

I have realized my problem. I always need someone to show me what's right, a role model, or else I will always feel inadequate. Sometimes I not only have to have one, I have to outdo them.

OMG, I forgot to tell you I was sitting at the bus stop and these way hot guys were about to go into "Big City Burrito," when 3 out of 4 were staring at me! Well then, this- weirdo Black old guy like talked to me and was way too creeped out to deal!!

Anyways more updates later.

Always

Alisa

**Undated**

I hate this place and I can't work on my issues with my mom if I can't see her. So screw y'all turning point. Lick my dick. I love my mom and I can't do anything to make her feel any better! Thank God she's coming tomorrow or I'd fuckin' scream. God damn Liz is getting on my nerves!! My mom, God I need her, but I don't want to need her! I don't!! Well, I'm going to read and then sleep so peace!!

Always

Alisa

**June 21st**

Screw this place in the ass!! I can't be here any longer!

Wow that was crazy. Roxy just pointed out to Ash-ley not to talk shit about me because I'm her friend. Well, Audrey jumped back and said you do to and Shantel and Veronica agreed. I'm alone. I'm very alone. My biggest fear is of being alone!

**June 22, 2003**

List of needs:

* Deodorant
* Toothpaste
* Toothbrush
* Rubber bands
* Tea for personal * Chapstick

**June 23, 2003**

7 days in June, 31 days = 38 days till August

I'm off house freeze tomorrow! Things are going to be okay. My time here keeps getting shorter! Shantel's going off again!! Hold on I need to go get the journal thing out of Angie's room. Wait till I tell you about Bitch ass Dandi.

**June 24, 2003**

Dang! IT'S FREAKING COLD OUT!

My teacher's back. I like her so much better than my other teacher. Yeah now I'm waiting for Desiral. She better hurry because I'm cold!! I need a cig too!

That was Courtney! I think I'm beginning to like her a lot more than I used to. But anyways,

There is this really hot guy in my class. I'm lookin' at him right now. Dude I was thinking about what it would be like to screw him during the damn movie. God damn I make myself horny. Anyways gotta get some shit done so peace!

Always

Alisa

**July 2, 2003**

Today I felt like learning about my D.O.C. Maybe I can do something to realize my behaviors in other areas. Jesus Christ this book is crazy.

"More, Now, Again" - Elizabeth

Wurtzel

Gotta go, but I'll be back.

Alisa

**July 8, 2003**

Special story from Sunday 6th.

Damn dude. Shit sure happens!! July 4, 2003 NO

FIREWORKS

Saturday (5th) Tanning and chillin' with Audrey. Then we met with this guy Joey, after drinking a bottle of Smirnoff. Then Sunday went to a meeting with Roxy. Good meeting!!

I liked!! Surfer Nick! Then about 6 pm (after going shopping with mom for a cute outfit for the club), Audrey picked me up and we picked up Roxy and met up with Audrey. We hopped in Audrey's car and drank. We ran out of alcohol fast so we had a bum buy us beer.

Budweiser baby!! Then we drank a few then off to the club. HOLLYWOOD LEGENDS***

It was so tight. Afterwards we left and stopped at Wendy's and asked for free food, but they ignored us, so we left and went to a 24-hour Taco Bell. They said, "come on inside," so we did. On the way, we got hit on by 2 other guys of cars! But we went inside and me, Audrey and Audrey flashed the Mexicans and got grips of food. They weren't all greasy dirty ones either.

Bitch Roxy kept says things like "How'd you like jail Alisa?" all because a damn cop kept driving around. Then she was calling me a hoe and a slut for talking to all those guys and flashing the Mexicans. Then she asks for some food. What the hell? She was also whining because she was late already when she had said she didn't care what time she got home!!

SCREW HER!

I'm the one that has friends to hang out with without sleeping with them. She screwed this guy and I'll mock on lots of guys at the clubs and she is calling me a hoe when I haven't got laid in 8 months. So screw her fat ass!! I don't need her! I have a meeting to go now, I don't need to go with her. I have friends!!

Anyways

Today I forgot to call right when I got there (to school) so I'm getting another SIR! How am I supposed to concentrate on school when I'm worried about getting back? That makes me not want to go back.

Well G2G

Always

Alisa

**July 9, 2003**

Another day at the Library!

**July 15th**

What is wrong with these people? Do your time that you have earned and then get out. Stop fighting, stop being dumb asses and pull your head out of your ass and come to realize that the world doesn't revolve around you!! Life is more than a damn' HALFWAY HOUSE. Get over yourselves!! Thank God for life!! But what am I gonna do when I get out?

Am I gonna go to school every day, will I ditch class, will I live to be 80? Will I get a good job? will I get a boyfriend? Or am I gonna get BORED and hate life?! I think, is what really scares me. Here I am making memories I will never forget, never. What if I don't ever have another great memory after I leave? In-tense question.

Always

Alisa

The following writings are directly from Alisa's journals and scrapbooks. I cannot be sure that all of these were written by her except the ones that she signed and dated. Some of the others may be the works of others that she took to heart. I have not put them in any particular order. I tried to group them by subject. By reading these, I hope that the reader will get an insight into what kind of tortured life Alisa led. There are many insights of what a person with bipolar disorder endures.

# *Dream*

Went with Debbie, Mom & Christy to stay at a mysterious new aunt's house for a weekend. Got there and they had an area out back where there was a door to the left and a door to the right. The left door led to a whole other house. The right door had a huge slide. But if you walked around the door there was nothing on the other side.

Inside the left door, there were like 15 rooms, 4 bathrooms and a huge living room. In between the rooms were couches and cushions with stairs between.

Then in the right there was like a slide that took you through a hundred different turns. When you started to think it would never stop, you hit a pit of balls.

Also, in the house there were a swimming pool with a dolphin and a room with three dogs in it and a cage with a rabbit.

Me, Debbie, and Christy went up to the house and found you sleeping, and my mysterious aunt gone. We woke you up and you said that you saw my aunt turn into an alien and put you to sleep. So, we all went to the house out back to be safe. The aliens were there and killed Christy. Then the aliens left. We stayed there and the aliens did not return, so we played with the animals.

I played with the dolphin and started getting really sick. Come to find Nikita (how did she get here?) has poured some-thing into the pool. I wouldn't leave the dolphin. You called a marine zoo person and the dolphin was saved.

I also wouldn't leave the bunny, so you let me take it home. On the way home, someone stopped us and tried to kill us but you pounded him and knocked him out.

In one of her journals—I feel like a unicon.

# *The Theater*

The laughter, the tears
The anger, the fears,
The excitement of the stage.
The lights, the praise, Line after line, scene after scene, and act after act.
That is on the front,
But behind the curtain, there is chaos and terror, Quarrel and threat.
Hatred is an enemy of the theater
But is there, always there
Ever watching for an opportunity to spring in the happy family of the theater.
So, beware, friends and family
Beware of hatred, for if it gets you
Then the saying "the show must go on"
Seems more terrible every time you hear it.

# *Nice Expressions to Describe Dumb People*

Not the sharpest knife in the drawer.
A few clowns short of a circus
A few fries short of a happy meal A few Cokes short of a six-pack.
A few peas short of a casserole
The wheel's spinning, but the hamster's dead.
One taco short of a combination plate.
A few feathers short of a whole duck.
All foam, no beer.
The cheese slid off his cracker.
Couldn't pour water out a boot with instructions on the heel.
He fell out of the stupid tree and it every branch on the way down.
An intellect rivaled only by garden tools.
As smart as bait.
Chimney's clogged.
Doesn't have all his dogs on one leash.
Forgot to pay his brain bill.
Her sewing machine is out of thread.
No grain in the silo.
Proof that evolution CAN go in reverse.
In the pinball game of life, his flippers were a little further apart than most.

# *Faith - Based Writings*

*The first part of this section came from what seemed to be an exercise that she must have done during one of her many rehabilitation stays.*

List the top five bad roots and fruits you selected. Next to each write the "good" fruit would be:

Rebellion and authority issues Good: Following the rules.

Manipulation

Good: Getting along with people without mind games

Drugs

Good: Drug Free

Pride

Good: Humble and modest

Self-centered

Good: Selfless

# *Written Prayer*

GOD, this is Alisa. I need help keeping inner strength, being positive, not falling into negative behavior. Let me realize the evil within myself and others. Let me realize who to help and who to avoid due to my own belief in you. Will you help me replace these with good things?

# *Life*

Darkened hearts and gorgeous arts, All a part of this world.
Happiness, greed, and people in need, All a part of this world. Death,
life, beautiful sites, All a part of this world. Love, respect, hell, and hate,
All a part of this world.
Family, friends, and fun that never ends,
Knowledge, privilege, sacrifice, Fruits of labor and lists checked twice,
Are all the benefits of life.
All That's Good and All That's Bad
Children sin, they just give in,
To what is called peer pressure.
She tries weed, her Dad did see,
And now he wants to crush her.
Another boy, he did destroy, Love and all that's good. Where's he now,
sitting downtown Killing in gangs of the hood.
Daddy yells and Mommy cries,
The daughter sits alone and sighs.
She doesn't understand, she doesn't care; She just has to realize.
That time goes by and yes it flies So don't let life just die.

# *Suicide*

You see him sit by himself
Like a long-lost teddy bear upon a shelf
Tears are always close to come,
He can't be happy when he wants to run.
He just feels hopeless and alone;
These feelings leave him extremely prone;
To being afraid
To run away
To leave fast and hide
But worst of all he's highly prone to what we call suicide.
So reach out, suicide is not joke!

# *Peace, Love and God!*

GOD

Green, orange, purple, blue.
Beautiful flowers that seem brand new.
New eyes, new soul, brand new heart.
That's where beauty has to start.
The sky, the trees, the mountains too.
All seem happier, brighter with you.
Beauty comes straight from within
So God, please help me be free of sin.
Help every day my life to begin.

# *Untitled*

God is the plan
God is interaction
God is everything that we do
God is the string of life that runs through us all
We are where we are
That's the perfect place to be
Pay attention and it's obvious
That everything is God
We just choose whether or not to pay attention.
*Found in her notebook but not written by her.*

# *A Teenage Prayer*

Everyday I look around
For the truth to be found
What lies ahead for me
What kind of person will I be
My imagination is running wild
Like an unburdened little child
There is so much inside of me
That is longing to be free
Sometimes I feel like I need to be led
There is so much confusion inside of my head
Put me on my appointed path
To be well-rounded and wise
Yet still continue to ask
Give me the words to know what to say
And the peace to know everything is ok
Let me have the ability to be strong and lead
And give people all the advice they need
Humbly I come, on my knees and pray
Because only you Lord, can show me the way.

# *A Dream of Love*

As the thunder rolls and the lightning strikes.
The light flashes and you're right by side.
I look outside and tornadoes are abroad.
The windows shatter and the trees look odd.
The day looks like night and the world looks scary.
I feel alone like a bush without a berry.
But there you, looking at me.
You give the courage to live and be free.
As we cuddle and I'm in your embrace.
Now I can stand up and laugh at the storm right in its face.
And just as my heart fills with joy
Like a child just given a brand-new toy.
My world seems to melt, and I start to scream.
I slowly wake up, tears, it was all just a dream.
Alisa
Feb. 12, 2003

# *The Tears I Cr y*

From experience do I speak
Of one who is weak, naïve, and sad.
As I lose one more piece of life
I don't know anymore what is truly right.
Expelled from school, from every job I was fired.
I am getting emotionally and physically tired.
Tired of people and sleepless nights
Tired of the system with all of their rights.
After it seems my bridges have burned
And nothing is left with everything yearned.
Every little thing seems like one more tear That drops to form my river of fear.
Crippled I am by my own faults
The pain and suffering never halts.
So the more I have begun to die The more tears I begin to cry.
And one time do I have to lie So I put on a smile and sing a little tune.
Because one day I will die too soon.
Alisa
Feb. 12, 2003

# *Untitled*

Love is real. It has to be. I love. I feel it in my heart. There just needs to be someone to exchange it with, shoot the shit, tell you never quit and never forget. Still dreams of you, wet…But I bet you're so set in your ways that my each and every day of efforts make no difference. That's why even though you were great, there's something better. Not the guy I dated before… no, no, wrong again. That bitterness is me, and that constant need to please, my sexy little tease. It's all mine, you will never take it, along with my pride, my swag, and all that you taught me. I refuse to give up, I don't need to tell me, I know.

Still invading my dreams and my daily thoughts despite how much medication and relaxation I dose up with. Is it heartbreak, a random mistake, internal outbreak of the inner self? I'm not the one who needs help. I'm not crazy, you're lazy. What happened to being treated like a lady? Now you are all shady because I'm not you're baby, a little too hazy, too fast for you. Good I hope you never catch up and just back up. Let me get my stacks back up. I'm no longer worried about <u>our</u> future plans, they are <u>mine</u>. I'm doing fine, finding my grind, with all the people you were too ungrateful and left them behind.

Now I'm leaving you too, mentally, physically, and emotionally. I'm officially done, lookin' out for number one. Fun? Have some, oh, right you can't, always looking over your shoulder. All the lies catch up and fester and you will be buried in your own fake reality you created. It's sad you actually believe it, but I'm done with you poser fairy tale that will never be real. You know what? I'm good now, I'm not perfect but worth it. I began to learn it, than serve it. I've heard the rumors and found humor in every situation. Funny, haha, never gonna put someone before my betterment. Ever again.

# *Don't Leave Me Alone*

I woke up this morning and was disappointed once again…
I can't seem to figure it out…
What am I doing wrong, am I taking the wrong path, the wrong route…
Then I saw you and your glowing smile, eye all alight.
And for the first time in a long time I believed in hope and life.
Then you kissed me and I melted.
The memory of past love hit me like a shooting star.
Now you are all I think about, whether you are close or afar.
My heartaches for you…
My body shakes for you…
And my soul yearns for you… What to do, what to do.
I have to have you for my own.
The light is once again shown to me
And I have to have you
So don't leave me alone.
I need you…

# *I Need You Now*

My love, I need you now
Please take me by the hand. Stand by me in my hour of need, Take time to understand.
Take my hand, dear love,
And lead me away from this place.
Chase away my doubts and fears, Wipe the tears from off my face.
Love, I cannot stand alone.
I need your hand to hold, The warmth of your gentle touch
In my world that's grown so cold.
Please be there for me
And hold me day to day. Because with your loving hand in mine, I know we'll find the way.
Love always
Alisa

# *My Love*

My love for you is ever changing
Growing each and everyday
We alone can face the world
So hand in hand we'll find a way.

# *Cocaine*

My name is cocaine, call me coke for short.
I entered this country without a passport.
Ever since, I've made lots of scum's rich.
Some have been murdered and others found in a ditch. I am more valued than diamonds, more treasured than gold Use me just once and you too will be sold.
I'll make a school boy forget his books,
I'll make a beauty queen forget her looks.
I'll take a renowned speaker and make him a bore.
I'll take your mother and make her a whore.
I'll make a preacher not want to preach.
I'll take your rent money and you'll be evicted.
I'll murder your babies, or they'll be born addicted.
I'll make you rob, and steal, and kill
When you are under my power, you have no will.
Remember my friend, my name is the big "C." If you try me one time you may never be free.
I've destroyed actors, politicians, and many a hero.
I've decreased bank accounts from millions to zero.
I make shooting and stabbing a common affair.
Once I take charge, you won't have a prayer.
Now that you know me, what will you do?
You'll have to decide, it's all up to you.
The day you agree to sit in my saddle,
The decision is one that no one can straddle.
Listen to me, and please list well,
When you ride with cocaine, you're headed for hell.

*This final writing is from a handmade birthday card Alisa made for me during the last years of her life. It is not dated so I don't know when she gave it to me, but it is the best card she ever gave me.*

Happy Birthday Mom!

I really think that even if I try my hardest (and I do) each and every day to make up for all the not so bright things in my life, I could never quite make it up…

But I'm sure going to try. I am the luckiest girl in the universe because my mom's love is unstoppable. I can even feel it from miles away and over the phone. You make me so happy just hearing your voice comforts me. Your embrace is Heaven on earth. Your proud smile towards me is motivation to keep moving up and never giving up. Thanks for everything you've done for me. I love you with all of my heart and I will spend the rest of my life trying to make you proud.

Happy Birthday Mom!

Always

Alisa

www.ingramcontent.com/pod-product-compliance
Lightning Source LLC
Chambersburg PA
CBHW032053020426
42335CB00011B/319
* 9 7 8 1 9 9 7 5 8 7 4 3 9 *